11.50

D112003

Beginner's Guide to Canoeing

Beginner's Guide to Canoeing

ALAN BYDE

PELHAM BOOKS

First published in Great Britain by PELHAM BOOKS LTD
52 Bedford Square, London, WC1B 3EF
FIRST PUBLISHED APRIL 1974
SECOND IMPRESSION DECEMBER 1974
THIRD IMPRESSION MAY 1977

ISBN 0 7207 0628 9

Printed in Great Britain by
Hollen Street Press Limited, Slough, Berkshire
and bound by Dorstel Press, Harlow, Essex

Contents

CHAPTER ONE

Why Go Canoeing?

There are as many different reasons for canoeing as there are canoeists, so the ideas in this book are offered as a matter of opinion, and personal observation. They are not necessarily correct, or a revelation of absolute truth; but they make an interesting story.

I started to build my first canoe, because I wanted to, when I was twenty-eight. My next-door neighbour and I had been going to evening classes each winter one evening per week and had made things in wood. So, when we saw a display of canoes made by people the previous year at the evening classes in canoe building in Durham, we did that instead. And having made the thing it became reasonable to learn to use it.

Looking back even earlier, perhaps the origin of the canoeing influence was a half hour in one on a sunny beach at Ganavan Sands, near Oban, when I was ten. Or, more probably, it was seeing a national canoeing event at Abbey Bridge, near Barnard Castle on the Tees. The canoes were brightly coloured, and swift and neat in their movements on the fast-running rapids. Sun and shadows under the trees on a lovely day, and that was certainly a pleasant experience. Since then I've been in a force eight off the Orme, and if it hadn't been for the fact I was scared to the roots of my being, it would have been cold, wet, and windy, apart from the noise. It was not pleasant. Each experience has its place in my recollection, as have the experiences of others new to canoeing.

I think, especially, of what happened when a child sat in a canoe for the first time. The day was warm, the sun shone. The first tentative prods with the paddle, and the canoe swung erratically out on to the river, the rippling water twinkling golden light on to the underneath of the echoing arches of the bridge. The eyes looked down into the water. The expression, as it is so often, was one of a slight wonderment, a gentle, happy expression. Paddling ceased, and still the interest in the surrounding water showed. This child, for all his life had been controlled in a dangerous world, by parents and teachers, admonished not to do this, and encouraged to do that. But now, sat in this shiny canoe, afloat somehow on this lovely water, he was not nagged at, not instructed – just drifting, watching, wondering. For some small time, perhaps the first time, he was master of his fate, captain of his soul.

Another child, vigorous, was a show-off to his pals, but listening, absorbed with restless energy everything he was told. He leaped into the canoe, grabbed paddle, and flailing the water like a lunatic, rocketed away from the landing to flip over, roaring with excitement, into his first capsize. Trudging wetly up the slipway, some of the first rush of excitement spent, he started again, and again.

I think of a man, approaching forty, with many experiences behind him. He knew water well, being a diver and swimmer, but he had never canoed before. He saw the new Eskimo kayak hanging in the workshop, being finished, and ready for the moulds to be taken off. There was a thoughtful expression, a deeper glint of understanding and intention, in his eyes. 'When you have finished this,' he said, 'what about me building one?' Later, in the pub, we talk about kayaks, and the remote lonely places around Britain's coasts where the traveller by sea can go in the kayak, the hunter's boat.

I remember, too, a woman, with a lively, interesting face, eyes twinkling, but with heavy legs and, as it turned out, arthritis of the hips. She was sixty-three, and had never canoed before. She wished to have a canoe and to learn to handle it so that she can watch the wild birds on the Cherwell. I built her a canoe, a lightweight, the colour she asked

8

for, and she calls it *Naiad* – a river nymph. One afternoon we went out on to the water near the Riverside Centre, of which I am Warden, and she followed my instructions so closely that it was as if my mind were directly co-ordinating her paddling.

She was concerned about what happens when it turns over, so over she went. Her awkward legs hindered her exit from the canoe, but out she came, startled, excited, determined. I didn't tell her, she told me: 'That wasn't very good. I must do it again.' And she did, three times in all. She'll be a long time living, that one, unlike some who start to die so young.

What is it that drives people to become involved in a nasty, cold wet and muddy sport like canoeing? Well it isn't always like that, but it can often be so. J.R.L. Anderson, boating correspondent of the *Guardian*, wrote a book he called *The Ulysses Factor* and in general examined what it is that drives people to sail alone around the world, to climb the Eiger, and so on. They all set out with great enthusiasm to come back to where they started, after having encountered great difficulties on the way. The thesis of the book, roughly, was that man has survived as a species for hundreds of thousands of years by striving, seeking, persisting in facing natural disasters, and still continuing. There is now built into his very soul a quality which is called the 'Ulysses Factor' in the book. Modern living protects many from natural disasters, and life can be quite comfortable, for those who are not simply subsisting. The need to express the factor that lies dormant in all to a greater or lesser degree is quite powerful and must out. So men and women cross the Atlantic singlehanded, just because it is there.

Some years ago, I was an assistant master in my first school, and the Headmaster, a tiny man who surrounded himself with big men as assistants, beamed up at me one morning as we proceeded into hall for prayers. 'What do you want to do with your life, eh, Byde?' he asked. Quick as a flash, for the answer leaped to the lips, I replied 'Die satisfied. Sir.' His expression of consternation was sheer joy for me. I never did do well at that school, except to leave it.

Satisfaction, now there is a word. So many young people tread tentatively a path set with hidden dangers, a life of nasty shocks and awful penalties for sins of omission or commission that really are given an importance that is out of proportion to their real seriousness. How pleasing, how satisfying, to do one thing that is right and sufficient in itself. No need to turn to others and ask, is it good? One knows it is good, and is satisfied.

What has all this to do with canoeing? Well, a personal philosophy is an inevitable thing as life develops. If one is thinking about it and weighing it, and selecting experience, then it could be that one is spending one's life in living as distinct from dying. Canoeing, walking mountains, sailing the Atlantic, watching wildfowl on a quiet river; there is something elemental about leaving the apparent safety of a warm home to seek the apparent danger of the natural places, unmodified by man. Mind you sometimes it is like putting on tight boots for the sheer joy of taking them off; perhaps we are all masochistic to some degree.

Apparent risk, and apparent danger. These are basic in the thinking which I apply to teaching young people, and older ones too, the pleasure of canoeing. On their second session, I take them over a little weir nearby. There are some weirs which are apparently dangerous, and others which are damnably dangerous, and I know now what the differences are. There is one thought which should engage your imagination. All water is potentially lethal, and between 750 and 1,000 people die each year in Great Britain in water accidents.

About fifteen to twenty-five are 'canoeists'. Of these, only two or three are experienced canoeists and these are generally trapped in some true accident, and those accidents are usually an accumulation of simple things which add up to disaster. If you want to avoid death by drowning, don't go near water. In the same vein, if you want to avoid dying, don't live.

There was a girl, sixteen, at Easter-time 1971. I had her in my group of ten youngsters, all about sixteen. She was very quiet all the time until she went over the weir, tight-lipped, white-faced, knuckles white, her expression one of resignation at the very last moment as the hull flipped over the top of the weir. Whumph! The canoe rocked and settled on an even keel below the weir. She looked at me with a curiously hard, penetrating look. Then her face changed, she whooped with exhilaration. She went on talking after that and took some stopping. Something changed in that girl that day.

Perhaps a conversation, purely imaginary I assure you, will explain more. 'Madam', I dream of saying, 'of course I guarantee to change your daughter. She will be in all ways a better person after I have finished with her. Safety? of course she will be perfectly safe here. Her character will blossom as never before, she will glow with an inner radiance.'

I could go on, but I feel twinges of revulsion. No one can guarantee that changes will follow from the practice of canoeing, either for good or ill, either in the body, mind or spirit of that person. What one can guarantee is that water is a lethal covering to the greater part of this world, and that some people will be stimulated to look outside their life so far and to rearrange some priorities they have had up to then. Whether they turn out to be better (i.e. more acceptable to others) or worse (i.e. less acceptable to others) as a result of canoeing experiences, only results will show, and all our futures are written in our pasts. I would like to think that, as a result of canoeing, most are given the opportunity to look again at living, and to change their way of enjoying life if they will.

Some changes can be impressive, such as that in a young man who was referred to me. He had a skin-head hair-cut, a lively manner and a slight sneer, he was sixteen, maybe seventeen, and he pitied me, apart from scaring me half to death by his potential for violence so clearly expressed. He wanted to build a canoe, which he nearly achieved with great energy and short enthusiasm. He brought along his elder brother in due course. 'Oh Lord,' thought I, 'another!' This one had very long hair and a saintly expression, and he tried hard to keep his cool. The skin-head had trouble on the buses, but he was provoked by the conductor, as well as being short-changed, and he was fortunate that some fellow passengers who knew him went to court to speak for him. At about this time, too, the elder brother was propelled violently through a large window and had some severe lacerations. No doubt you grasp the background. Two problems looking for somewhere to have an accident. That was two or three years ago.

Some time later, one summer at a beach in North Devon, with Atlantic surf creaming in around fifteen feet high, monstrous ground-shaking rollers, that trembled the air with constant thunder. As I walked on to the beach, I could hear wild shrieks coming from the surf about mid-beach, maybe quarter of a mile away. There in the surf, at one moment high in the air, then falling, tumbling over and over down a cliff of water to be overwhelmed, and yet to rise half a minute later from the welter whooping with sheer excitement, involved in the biggest scene of violence he had ever been in, was the skin-head. He struggled ashore soon after, his spray deck bashed in, the canoe waterlogged and scarred with compression cracks. But there were no people injured, no property (bar his own) damaged, which he could soon put right in the workshop, no victors and no vanquished in that battle. He was a very satisfied man that day, and the recollection still brings a thoughtful expression to his face. He is still an admirer of violence, and he met his very steady girl on the judo mat where her grading is better than his.

His brother, who tries hard to keep his cool and avoid trouble but finds it inevitably because his slightly hippy appearance, colourful and challenging, is a bit provoking to some locals. Even so, he is the one who takes youngsters camping, who drives an old lumbering mini-bus many miles, who looks after the youngster who has just unwisely consumed several pints of beer for the very first time. He canoes with skill, and can instruct with great calmness and thoughtfulness for the difficulties of others.

I don't guarantee that canoeing will always provide what the young person is looking for. But it can and does, sometimes.

CHAPTER TWO

Who Uses Canoes?

In the film, *Ryan's Daughter*, the opening shot was of a young woman on a cliff top and her parasol blows away down toward the sea; below is a curragh, and in it is the village priest and the village idiot. The place is the Cliffs of Moher, possibly the highest cliff in the British Isles. About seven miles out to sea is the isle of Inishere, one of the three Aran Isles. On the island, in the West Village, lives a man called Michie who makes the curraghs. He made me one, in 1969, and from the look of the few seen in the film, he made those too; the style is typically Aran. Those in the film were two-man curraghs, and mine is a three-man curragh, that is, made for rowing by three men.

It is not essential to be an idiot or to rely upon Heavenly

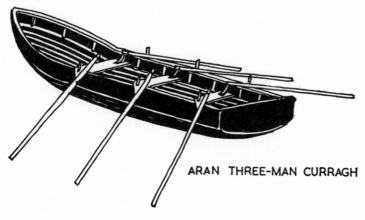

ARAN THREE-MAN CURRAGH

intervention to handle one of these boats; in fact the type of boat has been known since the Phoenicians traded in Britain long before the Romans came in 55 B.C. The curragh is based on similar shaped boats from Mediterranean countries.

In the South Atlantic, Tristan Da Cunha was the scene of a violent volcanic eruption some years ago: during the filming of the evacuation of the island several of the islands canvas boats were seen. They were built in much the same way as the curragh, and of the same materials. If you go North to Baffin Bay and land at an Eskimo settlement, you may, if the villagers are not engaged in drilling oil wells, find an old walrus hide covered boat called the 'umiak' (the 'women's boat'), which looks like a curragh. And on the north-east coast of Britain there are some beautiful boats called cobles. You can see them being made at Seahouses by the harbour, or at Berwick, and in fact anywhere along the coast where fishermen go fishing. They are made of wood and very solidly built to last many years and withstand great storms. But they are very much the same shape as the curragh, with high raking bow and a flattened stern to take the sand, so the boat sits level on the beach.

What, you may ask, has all this to do with canoes? The other Irish name for the curragh, which is commonly used, is 'Canoa'. The Spanish name for canoe is also *canoa* – a word that seems to have originated in Haiti, in the West Indies – and when the great storm scattered the Armada, it sent ships on the wings of the wind to be wrecked off Galway and Clare and Connemara. Besides the dead wrecks in the crevices of the reefs it seems to have left a few words still used in Ireland today. And although the designs seem to have evolved spontaneously, there is a remarkable similarity in the craft.

Other derivations of the curragh are suggested. Some think that they are elongated coracles made to carry heavier loads. In Ireland in Donegal there is, or used to be, the paddling curragh, which is paddled in the same way that a coracle is, and is clearly a stretched coracle. James Hornell wrote about them in 1937 in articles called *British Coracles and the Curraghs of Ireland*, reprints which are still available from the Maritime Museum, Greenwich, London, S.E.10.

The coracle is paddled by a single-bladed paddle, and it used to be made of wickerwork with a canvas cover proofed

TOWY CORACLE or CWRWC (COOROOK)

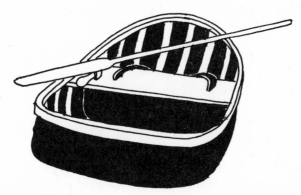

with pitch. It is one of the earliest forms of transport, having been used in Britain long before roads and bridges were made when coracles were carrying men to fish and people over rivers. Caesar's soldiers are reputed to have crossed a river in coracles made to the pattern seen in Britain, when on a campaign on the Continent. The North American Plains Indians had a boat called the bull boat, which was quite simply a coracle, round, with a buffalo hide covering with the hairy side outwards. Now how did they find out about the old British coracle? I think they simply developed it the same way that the old Britons did, because it is simple, easy

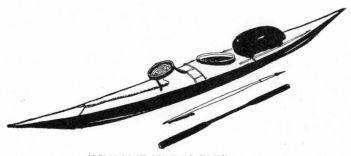

IGDLORSSUIT HUNTING KAYAK

to make from easily obtained materials, and is light to carry. A factory in Bridgnorth, on the Severn, was still making the coracles as an industrial venture in about 1900, and they were used as coal skips in small drift mines where iron rails and wheeled tubs would not go.

Whilst the coracle was being used all through the ages in Britain, and is still made and used both on the Teifi and at Ironbridge in Shropshire, Greenlanders were making their living by hunting seals and fishing. Two kinds of people lived in Greenland these being the nomadic Eskimoes and the settlers from Denmark, the Viking farmers. The nomads used a tiny craft, the kayak, which means 'the hunters boat'. It was not used for sport, but it has been described as a 'floating butcher's bench'. It carries a gun bag holding a shotgun and a .22 high-velocity rifle, near which is the club with which the animal is finally killed. There is a wide-bladed knife used for skinning, and the harpoon shaft and line pan. In front of that is a seal dodger, like a small square-rigged sail, which is designed to confuse the seal and cause it to think the advancing hunter and kayak is simply a drifting piece of ice.

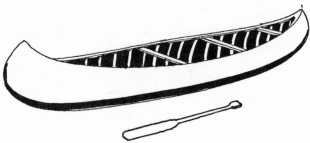

OJIBWAY INDIAN CANOE

The North American Indians also built floating craft, and these were the birch-bark canoes. It is probable that the Indians were originally of Asian stock, as are the Eskimoes, who crossed the Bering Straits and wandered through the land. I find it remarkable that one large land mass, and only the Northern part of that, produced two quite distinctive floating craft, the kayak, and the canoe, and from just these two basic types all our modern sporting canoes are derived.

Even modern canoeing is not so modern as you may think. John MacGregor is acknowledged as being the first man to make the lightweight canoe an internationally recognised sporting craft. That was in the 1860s, the then Prince of Wales gave Royal patronage to what is still the Royal Canoe Club. A book called *A Thousand Miles in a Rob Roy Canoe* was reprinted in 1963 (from the 13th Edition of 1881) by the British Canoe Union, and may still be available through your library. Meanwhile, the Americans were not far behind, and a man called J. Henry Rushton was building small rowing boats and special canoes to a pattern similar to the Rob Roy, for individual orders. The Adirondack Museum publishes a book by Atwood Manley called *Rushton and his times in American Canoeing*. This is also very informative about canoeing sport in the States and in Europe, in the latter half of the nineteenth century.

After the rather 'upper class' background of canoeing then, it lapsed into obscurity, and hitherto well-established canoeing clubs all over Britain simply faded away. About the 1920s, in Europe, a Danish businessman with contacts in Greenland, which is a Danish possession, brought back an Eskimo kayak and the knowledge of how to recover from a capsize by using the Eskimo roll technique. This knowledge spread, and in addition to the few straightforward sprint events for kayaks in regattas, and the few sailing canoe races, an opening was made for white-water (a stretch of river, or surf, where the water flow is broken and the surface appears white) and sea canoeing. Self-rescue by rolling was a very appealing form of exercise. So the nature of sporting canoeing began to change. The new sport of slalom started about 1938 in Germany, was revived after the war, and is now a very attractive and colourful sport for the many.

During the war the value of the kayak was recognised for military use – as sea-going and river transport for soldiers laden with explosives – and the story of the *Cockleshell Heroes* by C. E. Lucas-Phillips has been told in film and book. This type of heroism had a striking effect on the imagination of many people.

After the war there developed the Outward Bound Schools, based on the teaching of Dr Kurt Hahn. These schools challenged young people to reach deep into their reserves of resolution and determination, and through adventure to discover more about themselves. The canoe and kayak offered useful vehicles to set up the situations which offered the challenges. Outdoor Activity Centres followed, run by the Central Council for Physical Recreation, and by Local Education Authorities and these also offer canoeing. In fact in 1966 I found that of over thirty Outdoor Activity Centres, only three did not offer canoeing, and that canoeing was as popular as rock climbing and mountain walking, leaving many other sports well behind.

Subsequently to this development, and with the advent of glass-reinforced plastics (G.R.P.) in canoe building, many schools have been able for the first time to build and maintain a good fleet of sound, up-to-date canoes for young people to use on local ponds, canals, rivers and swimming pools. Meanwhile open canoe clubs were building up all over Britain, and the British Canoe Union shows a rapid growth each year.

The British Canoe Union started early in the Thirties; it had previously been a small association of six canoe clubs which included the Royal Canoe Club and the Canoe Camping Club. Now it is a complex grouping of specialist and general interests. The Council includes the Sprint and Long Distance Racing, Touring, White Water, Slalom (a competition, on a white-water river, where artificial obstacles in the form of hanging gates make the competitor's task more difficult). Sailing (racing) and Coaching Committee representatives. A Canoe Polo Committee has also been formed. In addition to the B.C.U. there is the Army Canoe Union, the R.A.F. Canoe Club, and the Royal Navy Kayak Club. The Scots have their own Scottish Canoeing Association which organises its own coaching and qualification schemes, as do the Army and other groups, and all these qualifications are similar. The Northern Ireland Canoe Club also is a growing organisation.

Access for canoeists to much of England and Wales' rivers

is restricted by angling pressure groups, and this pressure is increasing. It is going to be difficult to launch a canoe on inland waters soon, unless some reasonable agreement on access can be negotiated. The most hopeful possibility is that Access Sub-Committee of the B.C.U. and the National Sports Council and the various angling and land-owning representative bodies may eventually produce a useful and respected system. The only way that the individual canoeist can affect these decisions reasonably is to join the B.C.U. and lend his help to the work, simply by being a member at the very least.

Decisions in the courts have been handed down in the last few years. The interpretations have been quite different. Briefly, each river and each use of that river offers its own problems. The decision on the Wharfe was at first against canoeists, then for them on appeal, and then against them at a higher court. A decision on the Spey, concerning the use of the river by an outdoor activities centre run by Clive Freshwater, was in general for the canoeists, but this was conditional on sensible use and exercise of the right to use what was held to be an existing navigation. The message as I see it is that angler and canoeist must learn to compromise. Neither is utterly free to use a river as he pleases.

CHAPTER THREE

What Is A Canoe?

Way, way back when Adam was a lad, it is reasonable to suppose that some prehistoric people straddled a fallen tree and moved it somehow to the other bank of a river. Later they found ways of making a floating object without first using suitable trees. Quite possibly the coracle, a sort of large basket, would be woven from withies and covered with animal hides, and proofed with grease.

Among the North American Indians, each tribe and each canoe builder developed an open canoe made usually from birch bark, now known as the 'Canadian canoe'. Differences in decorations, shapes, styles, and so on became obvious, so that a knowledgeable student of these types of boats could recognise the origin of each one, and possibly who built it. Edwin Tappan Adney, an American with time and money to explore that great continent, set out to see and measure and comment upon every type of canoe, and later kayak, that he could find. Howard I. Chappelle, of the Smithsonian Institution Department of Transportation, worked on Adney's notes, and with observations of his own, there was published the magnificant reference work *The Bark Canoes and Skin boats of North America*. In it are full details of what an eskimo kayak is and what a canoe is.

Dimensions are of interest. The 'average' kayak illustrated in Adney and Chappelle's book is seventeen feet by twenty-two inches. The canoes illustrated in that book vary greatly in size from tiny ten-foot boats up to Hudson Bay load carriers. These boats, used by the French 'voyageurs', were paddled by ten men and could carry loads of several tons; the length and beam might be forty feet by six feet. The coracle, however, is usually about four feet by five feet, and about fifteen inches deep. But even that will carry about a quarter of a ton. A larger type of 'coracle' called a 'quffa' has been seen, with diameters of up to sixteen feet, used in the shipyards and ports in the Mediterranean, and in the region of the Tigris and Euphrates rivers a craft of the same shape is woven of basket material and made watertight with pitch. Such boats were used to carry shipyard equipment and were made of reeds bound into great flat baskets of great diameter, much in the same way that the papyrus craft *Ra* was made for Thor Heyerdahl's Atlantic crossing.

In the Pacific, the Maoris of New Zealand have vast war canoes, hewn from one great trunk of a tree, cut in remote parts of the forests and carried on rollers to some special beach, where it is given its purposeful shape.

Variations on the essential purity of the kayak have been seen. In the Kuril Islands off Asia, and then across the Aleutian chain of islands, the Russians pursued the fur trade with great enthusiasm, and developed links with the Eskimo fur seal hunters. The boats that the Russians used were small wooden sailing traders, but to go ashore in places where no harbours existed required still smaller craft. The kayak was about the right size, but it had only one hole for the paddler. So longer kayaks, with two and even three holes, were built. This type was called the baidarka, and in 1962 an American produced a set of drawings for such a three-holer, drawn from the original, but intended for sporting use.

It is interesting to follow basic designs through to modern types, and perhaps to reverse the process. You may disagree with the analysis which follows, and if so, I hope you will let me know.

Every boat floats by displacing water, and the skin boat does it by having a skin waterproofed by fats or pitch, which is pushed down into the water by a framework of springy woodwork, or stiff grasses. Braced across this framework of springy wood is a seat, and this in turn carries the weight of the paddler. The load may be carried by a little platform fixed to the bottom. In this case the mechanical strength of the whole is provided by the framework, and the spaces between the frames is filled by a skin stretched across the framework, and this keeps the water outside the boat. By a steady branching out of structure, from seat to strut, frame and stringer, the weight of the paddler is shared out fairly evenly over a soft skin which is holding out the water.

The following types of boat satisfy this analysis: The coracle – hides and skins and withies. The Eskimo kayak – skins or canvas, over stringer and frame. The modern touring canoe – plasticised canvas over stringer and frame. The ultra-lightweight slalom boat – an extraordinarily thin glass-resin flexible laminate, held in place by a diamond lattice of carbon fibre laminated in with the glass.

Alternatively, there is the monocoque structure. The canoes which use this type of construction are made of glass-reinforced plastic, or of plywood sheets tied with wire and sealed with resin and glass strips; both are modern types. I first learned of this as a boy during the war when I heard that the Spitfire was an alloy monocoque structure, unlike the Hurricane which had a frame over which alloy panels and proofed canvas were fixed. The modern car is a monocoque structure, where the body shell carries the loads and stresses of the vehicle and its use. Earlier cars and more expensive cars have a chassis, over which a frame is built on to which are fixed panels, wings (or fenders) windscreens (or windshields), and so on. As mentioned, the modern technique of using glass-fibre sheets bonded together with synthetic resins has led to the development of canoes of monocoque shell construction. However internal frames in a glass-reinforced plastic (G.R.P.) structure are usually a source of trouble, because stresses are concentrated there and stress concentration gives rise to shattering of the laminates around the points of attachment to the internal frames. Modern advanced technology has given us very strong carbon fibres, and when these are laminated into the boat, the shell thickness may be reduced as it is no longer carrying the load; most of the stress is now contained within the carbon fibres. However, the flexing of the panels between the carbon fibres leads to shattering around the line of the carbon strands. So the ultra-lightweight canoe is possible, but it doesn't last very long. Until carbon fibres are produced in a woven cloth at a price which makes it possible for manufacturers to produce ultra-thin and very light waterproof laminates, they present more problems than help for the modern competitive canoeist. Ultra-light canoes have been made down to 18 lb. weight, but 25–30 lb. for a G.R.P. solo canoe/kayak is about right for reliable use.

In the historical line of monocoque boats I would list the following : The Maori war canoe – solid hewn tree trunk. The medieval dug-out in Britain, or any early social organisation. The modern G.R.P. canoe/kayak. Vacuum-formed plastic boats, dinghies, canoes/kayaks (not successful as yet in canoes/kayaks).

The North American Indian canoe is a little difficult to place. The birch bark shell is stiffened internally with long slats added after the skin has been formed on a building base (unlike the kayak, which has its skin attached to a framework which is first built from wood). The canoe slats are then internally ribbed to provide extra strength. It is probable that the canoe is more of a soft skin and frame type than a monocoque structure.

Looking into the principle of what we do to a person when he is in a boat, we have given him the means to displace water without being in contact with that water. He doesn't get wet. Also, the human form is not a good water shape for speed or manoeuvring. It is a most adaptable shape, but it doesn't go quickly through the water. So the body in a boat has a better shape for the business of moving about on the water. The boat may also provide protection against physical contact with rocks, as when shooting rapids.

Developing this idea further, what we are doing is packing people for the water. The study is not canoes, or kayaks, but rather packing cases. With, say, polystyrene foam plastic blocks, one may protect a refrigerator, or T.V. set from damage on the way to the customer. So we pack the canoeist. Why not take a block of foam, say fourteen feet long, two feet wide, and about a foot deep, and shape it outside like a canoe, and inside like a person? Then we have a solid boat which could do the job. However, standard packing case foam is very friable, liable to crumble when struck hard.

If the foam can be made tougher without much of an increase in weight, then we have a better material. This has been done with high density polystyrene foam, polyethylene foam, polythene foam . . . the list is considerable. However, most of these foams permit water absorption. A lightweight foam boat with a tough skin is a possibility, but here we have style and fashion against us. The high-class competitive canoeist is either in an ultra-lightweight G.R.P. shell, or a beautiful veneer laminate, hot-moulded racing boat. Carving the foam to shape as with custom-built Malibou boards is a possibility, but no one to my knowledge has done it yet, and really cheap machine-pressed and moulded foam boats will depend on a bigger market than seems at present to exist in Britain. However, to be able to buy a large foam blank roughly cast to the shape required, and then to work on it with rasp and sandpaper to get the required individual shape, then to skin it with a plastic from a spray-on bottle would really open up the possibilities for do-it-yourself boat designing.

Another type of boat is used, and it derives its rigidity from air pressure differences. A shaped and inflatable bag is, when pressurised to about 2 lb. per square inch, a useable canoe. It consists of a series of tubes, rather like an air bed, which together take up the shape required, with inflated transoms and thwarts. These types have been very successful as planing speed boats for rescue and escort work on beaches, and so on. But the canoes lack the colour of resin and the glitter of the highly-polished G.R.P. shell, and the shape is a bit indeterminate. The boat is not really rigid, it carries a lot of windage usually and so blows about the sea. It weighs very little, so it is attractive in that respect for the small child. These toys that one sees at beaches could be termed do-it-yourself-destruction kits, but if ever some ace canoeist wins a world championship in an inflatable, then we may see some development of that type. A historical list of these types would include :

The air-filled animal skin. A photograph facing page 449 in the October 1971 issue of the *National Geographic Magazine* shows an Indian using this means for getting about on water.

The inflatable canoe, usually to be seen in the lists of European inflatable craft manufacturers. British manufacturers seem not to bother much with this type.

Since this book was written, I have been introduced to the surf ski. It is a craft which I at once labelled the Dinosaur – too big, too old, too heavy, and horribly ugly. Since then, improved models from Australia have become available, and I have been able to bring kayak design to these boats with some success. The British National Champion in 1976 paddled one of my skis in the Surf Lifesaving Association of Great Britain National Finals at Bude. A variety of types exist, basically one sits on a recess in the deck, rather than in a cockpit. Imagine if you can a surfing K1, unsinkable provided it is not holed or torn apart by surf. Between one's thighs there stands what we call the ski tree. By gripping with the thighs, one stays on through loops and rolls and the thrashing of the surf. Exit is instant by releasing the grip of the thighs. Benefits, no capsize panics; novices can be sent out on moderate surf with no instruction at all, except to keep away from swimmers and other surfers; no spray decks to trap, or fray, or rot. The footrest bar is open for adjustment; no possibility of being trapped within the cockpit. People have died in kayaks, trapped for one reason or another underwater. Mind, for a long journey I still want a nice cosy cockpit.

So, what is a canoe? Well, it's a kayak and a coracle, it's a water shape for a person using the water, it's a packing case it's rigid or floppy, long and thin or circular, made of modern plastics and ancient trees and animals. It is for trade, hunting, sport, a work bench and a war vessel. It is for children to play in and for men to win World Championships in. It is seen on all the seas and on rivers, canals and ponds, swimming baths and fiords. It is folk art and a stripped tool or weapon.

One is tempted to enquire, how long is a piece of string?

CHAPTER FOUR

Which Canoes And Equipment Will Suit My Needs?

When a paddler is in his canoe, several items have been brought together and assembled into a unit suitable for a purpose. These are, roughly:

Person
Clothing
Canoe
Paddle
Lifejacket
Crash Helmet
Spray Deck
The Water in use
Purpose

PERSON

This section on the person helps to assess what one's needs are. Some may need the catharsis of a crisis in the spirit, some may need quite simply the healthy physical exercise to be happy; others may love the instant reactions that white water sport and slalom may demand, the decision-making that takes a gate one way rather than another. All these aspects affect the canoeing into which one goes.

A person may be thought to be composed of three essential parts, each intimately interlinked, interdependent, inseparable.

There is the human body. Is it strong enough, well enough, warm enough? Is muscular co-ordination good enough? Can it see where it is looking, listen to what it hears?

There is the mind. Is it a thinking mind, able to take in

impressions, assess them, and give effect to them through the motor nervous system? Is the mind stable enough in its thinking, effective in action and reaction? Has it a suitable store of experience on which it may draw; have enough conditioned reflexes appropriate to the practice of canoeing been built into the mind-computer?

And there is the spirit. This is the essential person, and all that the mind and body can do is to some extent modify the expression of the spirit. If the spirit is enduring and inclined to keep on keeping on, that person is one of nature's survivors. Every spirit reaches breaking point from time to time, and this can happen whilst canoeing. Recovery is either a matter of living with the scars, crippled within, or strengthened by the effort of will needed to survive and still to continue to enjoy life. What one has been is altered by one of these crises, and there is no guarantee that past experience will help. The crisis may be the first capsize, or it may be a thundering welter of water in a tide race off a great cliff, against which the gale hurls spray and roaring waterspouts.

CLOTHING

Clothes are used to cover us and to keep us at a suitable body temperature. Clothing incorporates style, fashion, impression, suitability for a purpose. One thing I was told long ago, is, if it looks right, it very probably is right. Dress for the job, look the part, and maybe you can do the job. Canoeing being the nasty wet, cold, muddy sport it is, one finds that clothing is very practical. Its first purpose is to keep one warm whether wet or dry. It must not hinder movement, nor must it be so baggy that water can swill around inside and thus carry away body heat. Air bubbles can be trapped within loose clothing, and in a capsize, this free air may be squeezed up to one's ankles, where the trousers are tucked into socks. This forms a buoyancy aid for the feet, yes, but this keeps one's head underwater rather forcefully. Loose clothing can become caught in odd pieces of the canoe, and hold one in the upturned canoe.

The clothing should be fairly close fitting, but not tight. The arms and shoulders have need of gross movements, but

RECOMMENDED CLOTHING : FAIR WEATHER

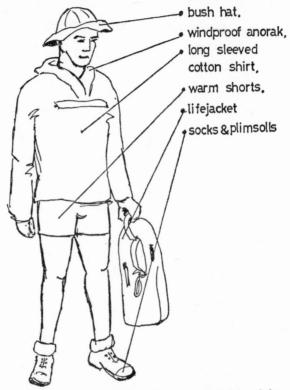

- bush hat.
- windproof anorak,
- long sleeved cotton shirt,
- warm shorts,
- lifejacket
- socks & plimsolls

the legs are fairly still. Close-fitting and fairly tight clothes around the legs, such as wet suit trousers are good. Feet, if cold, are (one might say) a 'pain in the neck'. Keep the feet warm with a pair of wet-suit boots, or good woollen socks and plimsolls. These days the prevalence of broken glass causes one to take care not to cut the feet, so wear plimsolls with good soles, even if the uppers are holed. The body, chest, and shoulders should be covered by a windproof anorak. This is the bit of you that sticks out into the windflow, and its the rate of loss of heat to fast-moving air that causes severe chilling, even in summer, especially if the body is wet.

The pectoral muscles are usually rubbed by the overlying clothing because it is pressed on to the body by the lifejacket.

If the clothing around the chest is neoprene rubber, it will very soon chafe the skin and cause quite painful sores. I find that a good cotton shirt, with a woollen jumper over it, or perhaps the nylon-fur polar suit type of thing is ideal if covered with a *windproof* nylon anorak. Waterproofing is an unrealistic aim in modern canoeing, as one is quite likely to be completely submerged several times in the average day, as skill and ambition progress. However, a windproof anorak with a shiny outer surface, proofed nylon, or even a wet-look raincoat would do very well. The essential thing is, that the airflow around the part of the body which protrudes from the shelter of the canoe should not cause water to evaporate and thus carry away heat by evaporation, which is a very serious source of heat loss.

Bearing in mind that any clothing worn is going to be wet, then it should be easy to spin dry and so get rid of the water. River and sea water are both living with bacteria, which if left in damp clothing give rise to the saying, 'Old canoeists never die, they only smell that way'. Canoeing clothing must always be rinsed in clean water and dried. Also, the human animal being what it is, it perspires, especially if covered in windproof covers, and the inside of the cover becomes beaded with condensed sweat.

Heat loss is energy loss, and a full day's canoeing is very demanding, in that energy expenditure is always being demanded, but feeding to replace it is not easy and is often impossible. Therefore if energy is conserved by keeping heat loss to a minimum, the body has more energy available for the muscles to work. It is said that about a third of the body's total heat loss is from the shoulders, neck, and head, so it is a good idea to keep these covered. However, at the start of the day the body starts to burn energy and give off a lot of heat, so a good way to stay comfortable, even though tending to overheat, is to expose the head and neck to the air around, remembering to cover up later when heat production is being curtailed. I remember once when cycling that I had a persistent slight headache, but I was warm on a cold winter day out on the moors. It was only in the mid-afternoon that I realised that my shirt collar was rather tight and was pressing gently on my neck. I realeased that and the headache went, but I was less warm.

When canoeing, the hands must hold the paddle, and without that one is truly 'up the creek'. If the hands are really cold they have no sensation, and whilst the power of the grip is supplied by muscles in the forearm, if touch is lost, grip becomes uncertain. The hands are usually left exposed by canoeists, because to muffle them is to reduce accuracy of feel of the paddle shaft. Even so, on really cold days the canoeist may well wear, ideally, thin silk gloves covered by thin neoprene kitchen gloves, not tight, but close fitting. Incidentally, paddling style is very important in keeping the hands warm. Learn good style, such as the racing men use, and your hands will keep warm. If you seize hold firmly and grip the shaft with a white-knuckled grasp, then your hands will quickly cool off because the continuous pressure reduces the volume of warm blood which is able to circulate. A relaxed muscular action, however, assists in pumping blood through the arteries and veins.

CANOE

The canoe must satisfy many needs. Basically these needs can be listed as follows, without any conclusions. One quality is contrasted with its opposite across the page.

High speed forward	Manoeuvrability
Lots of room inside	Seaworthiness
Stable on flat water	Stable on rough water
Difficult to overturn, flat water	Easy to roll
Easy to keep in straight line	Easy to turn
Suitable for playing in	Suitable for journeys
Suitable for a big man	Suitable for a small child
Suits the pocket	Suits its purpose
Durable	Lightweight
Home-made	Resale value
Sea-going	Rough rivers
Polo canoe	Never damaged
Folding canoe	Inexpensive
Heavy and durable	Easy to carry
and so on ...	

Which Canoes and Equipment Will Suit My Needs?

My instructor's canoe weighs about forty-five pounds, and I flip it lightly over my shoulder . . . I really do, there is a knack in it. It doesn't bother me, unless it must be carried more than fifty yards, which is when I would prefer a lightweight about half the weight. A lady of mature years once wished to know more about canoeing, so I asked her to pick up one of the Centre boats, to see if it would suit her for weight. She pulled, and subsided on to the canoe. So I built one for her that weighed about twenty-eight pounds, and that she could manage.

I'm fairly hefty, and although I wouldn't call my bulk vast, it is not inconsiderable. There is one design of canoe into which I pop with ease, and it is a snug fit. A tall, rangy lean man, a teacher near by and a one-time rowing man, tried it, and although of the greyhound breed, could not get in.

One of the stunts which designers pull on small people, who are usually children, is to design a small canoe, especially for the kiddies, then fit it with a full-size cockpit for the average man so that it will appeal on two counts, one to the child, and one to the adventurous dad with a small child; they both can use it. It's like the Christmas Day 'Dad, please may I play with my train set?' It's my firm belief that small people should have canoes especially made for them, so that they suit them as adults are suited. No temporising with dual-purpose cockpits where junior rattles down the rapids like a pea in a pod. In a capsize he doesn't get out, he falls out.

PADDLE

The kayak paddle must be the right length. Most people measure this by standing upright with one arm raised almost to full stretch. The paddle stands upright beside one foot, and the raised arm should just be able to curl the fingers over the paddle tip. This is about 7 ft. 2 in. for the average 5 ft. 10 in. man. Novice's paddles need a simple arrangement of alloy shaft with plastic sheathing and flat plywood blades stuck into the ends. Next come wooden laminated paddles, all one piece, with curved blades, and costing about four times the basic paddle. Then, even further up the scale, come the top-class racing and sprint paddles, spooned, beautifully balanced, costing about six times the basic paddle. Recently in Britain we have been getting inexpensive moulded A.B.S. flat paddle blades with alloy shafts from the U.S.A.; I have seen two types, one with a very small diameter paddle shaft, quite unsuitable for real canoeing, but the other is just about right, with a shaft diameter of about $1\frac{1}{4}$ in., and the blades seem indestructible. The trouble is, the shafts may take in water and then if sufficiently waterlogged will sink. One quality of a paddle must be that it floats, so that it can be picked up when needed. Finally, whilst I am quite happy to share my canoe with anyone who wants to use it, I am very reluctant to allow anyone to use my paddles. Paddles are very much more personal than the canoe is.

The true canoe which uses the single-bladed paddle is the Canadian type, but it is remarkable how similar, making allowances for body size, that single-bladed paddles are all over the world. Basically the single-bladed paddle should stand as high as the tip of one's chin or nose; somewhere between the two will do fine. The ratio of shaft length to blade length should be about $3:2$. If the paddle is five units long, then the shaft should be three units long and the blade two units long. The coracle paddle, the North American Indian paddle, the paddles from the Maori war canoes, paddles from the Amazon, all of these fit very closely within the limits described. There is something rather awe-inspiring about this certainty of similarity in such basic matters as making water craft move. If you should be in Oxford, go to the Pitt-Rivers museum and see these for yourself.

LIFEJACKET

Once this section would have begun: 'whilst with me you will always wear one', and that would have been the end of the Section. Now I know that the use of the lifejacket is subject to many decisions which depend on many influences. Some of these are discussed in this section.

Some years ago I was asked to determine the facts of a drowning. A boy, a good swimmer, was shooting a small weir and he was wearing a good lifejacket, properly adjusted.

The weir was in flood, and the water turbulent. The canoe capsized. The boy was caught in the return flow under the weir, and he was driven down by the downflow from the weir, and pushed away underneath. The lifejacket then exerted its lifting force and brought him up a few yards from the weir, but in the returning surface flow which sent him back into the downflow from the weir. The policeman who recovered the body said that he went down, was under for 4–5 seconds, then re-appeared for 2–3 seconds, then down he went again, in a steady rhythm.

Over and over he tumbled, to drown in confusion. The lifejacket cannot be blamed, it did its job . . . but sometimes one must go deep and escape by going underneath the turmoil, and a lifejacket will not permit this. Another similar disaster soon after caused the standard for the British lifejacket to British Standard Specification 3595 to be altered and the total buoyancy reduced.

BSS 3595 Two stage	Buoyancy Aid Waistcoat	Buoyancy Aid Air pillow	BSS 3595 Inflatable (gas bottle)
£12 Uncomplicated Bulky	£10 Simple Flat Warm	£4 Cheap Light	£16 Complicated Unobtrusive

My choice

A lifejacket should have the majority of its buoyancy in front on the chest so as to provide a turning moment to bring the floating body face uppermost. The head should be prevented from lolling sideways or backwards by a buoyant neck piece. Provided that the mouth and nose are kept above water at all times, one need never fear drowning. However, the first capsize removes that attempt to keep safe, and so one must learn to hold one's breath, an unnatural act requiring education.

Many aids to buoyancy for the body are in the form of waistcoats and have neck and arm holes, with much of the buoyancy evenly distributed around the chest. They are often zipped up the front to aid ease of putting it on, but once, when I had to hurry to help someone at the surf championships, I could not get the zip to unjam, and fortunately someone else was not so slow as I. A lifejacket with popper studs at the sides may be better than a zipped or maybe laced-up waistcoat type; (one loses the lace).

A lifejacket to BSS 3595, or, for example, one of a similar type which the Navy issues to Sea Cadet Units, has numerous straps and loops and buckles. These can catch in the branches of overhanging bushes in a flooded river. The trapped body would then oscillate, and the rate of this would be some product of the springiness of the branch, and rate of flow of the water, the weight of the person and the drag of that body in the water. Certainly regular total immersion in a steady rhythm would ensue. Given that one can release the trapped buckle, this releases the body to drift into the next entanglement. The waistcoat type buoyancy aid does avoid that type of trouble, as it does not have any straps.

Another function of the waistcoat type is to keep the body warm by insulation, and this it does. This is a not insignificant part of its life-keeping quality. If one is warm, one can think and act. If a person is very cold, it may be that the ability to think is very much reduced and the ability to act almost nil. A further useful point about the waistcoat type is that, if one is swimming in a rough river, it can reduce bruising and maybe rib breakages by cushioning the rib cage against impact with rocks and obstacles. I must say I never heard yet of anyone with rib breakages as a result of swimming in a rough river, and banging into rocks.

However, given the awful day when I must answer to the coroner, the question: 'What did you do for this young person, Mr Byde?' I may have to think very hard before saying with conviction: 'I advised him not to wear a lifejacket, Sir.' Or, 'He was wearing a buoyancy aid, not a lifejacket to BSS 3595.'

Taken overall, it is safer to wear the lifejacket to BSS standards and to stay away from dangerous places if in charge of a group of people whilst canoeing. If you are making your own decisions, as an independent person, then you have these choices :

No lifejacket at all

A buoyancy aid

A deflated jacket to BSS 3595

An inflated jacket to BSS 3595

Each one of these decisions, given a time and place and a person has its good points and its bad points. Experience will inform you, and this book may help.

CRASH HELMET

This is clearly to keep your head from being banged about, and so causing loss of sensibility. I have worn one many times and it has been of use twice, in each case in the same way. I slipped when hurrying on wet, flat and weedy rocks by a river, and my feet shot out in front and my head cracked against a sharp shelf of rock, with no bad effects. However, when on the sea in strong winds, anything from force four upwards on the Beaufort scale, the slots in the helmet (through which the water spills when rolling) act as organ pipes, and the resultant howl of wind and the blanket of roaring sound is very wearying in the long run, and quite worrying. In a force eight gale in these conditions the noise rose to the threshold of pain, prolonged, unremitting, constant. That was a difficult trip.

None the less, the helmet is a must in most advanced canoeists' kit, and for many novices the need for a helmet is there from the beginning. I remember a deep water rescue just offshore in which I was trying to clamber up between two canoes, mine and the helper's, and they swung together on the wave surge with a great bang across my ears, and I was knocked quite dizzy for a moment. A helmet then would have been a great help. The usual helmet is that used by ice hockey players, which is made from plastic. It is light, floats, and is inexpensive, costing about the same as the cheaper paddles. One activity for which the helmet is a must, and is laid down in the rules, is canoe polo. During a vigorous game the paddle blades and arms and bodies (and dare I mention fists), can cause a temporary disorientation in a ringing head.

Spray Deck

This is a soft material, waterproof, with elastic edges, which seals to the cockpit rim and to the middle of the body. Its purpose is to keep the wet out. In many canoeing actions it must accommodate to gross body movements, so its design is rather critical. It must have release tabs or straps on it, as in a capsize and failure to roll, it may be that the pressure differences between the inside of the spray deck and the outside, now under water, are enough to cause the spray deck to seal tight and become almost immovable. If this happens, it is impossible to get out until the pressure difference is released by the entry of water, so as to allow the extraction of the lower part of the body from what is really very similar to a sealed bottle. The water, or air, can get in either by lifting the spray deck edge with the release strap or tab; by ripping the material; by wrenching the cockpit rim out of the deck; or by splitting the deck away from the hull. I have seen every one of these things done, and I have been so trapped myself, so I know where people without access to air get the power to cause such serious damage to a canoe. But this is a very rare happening and proper design, construction, instruction and experience will avoid any serious difficulty.

The Water In Use

The type of canoe, and consequently equipment, is dictated by the water one may use. For example, many schools may have access to a swimming pool, say 25 yards long, in which canoe polo would be an ideal way to keep vigorous young people energetically involved. In that case I would, given a life saver in charge as a referee, require polo canoes, plus spray decks and paddles and helmets. Nothing else would be necessary.

A person wishing to canoe competitively would need the

right equipment, of a quality rare and expensive and backed by knowledge won only after years of experience.

A novice canoeist on a river such as the Thames, which is flat between locks, could get away with a straight running canoe, no spray deck, no helmet, a suitable paddle, and a lifejacket. However, he would need to know where the weirs were, and which ones are boat wreckers, potential killers, and which are fun and exciting to play with. Two such weirs run within fifty yards of each other a half mile from my Centre; one has wrecked two boats and one is fun.

A novice by the sea with solely the sea to start on is in a

INTERNATIONAL
SAILING CANOE

very demanding position, but the satisfaction to be derived in due course is very considerable. It is impossible to name a canoe type or design as being suitable for this or that, as always someone will turn up with a quite untypical but satisfying use of that craft. Canoeing has a dozen different branches, a thousand different waters, and many scores of old and new designs, all of which are suitable for something. The only reliable way to gain experience quickly, avoiding the worse dangers, is to join an established club. No matter how daft you may be, you can guarantee someone has already done a dafter thing.

PURPOSE
I think I must have covered nearly all the purposes for which canoes or kayaks can be used, so far as we know at present. I'll list them :

Canoe touring, rivers
Canoe touring, sea
Baths training, rolling practice
Canoe polo
Canoe slalom
Long-distance racing
Sprint racing, local events
Sprint racing, Olympic class
Canoe Sailing IC.10
White water racing
Surfing
Beach and Surf rescue unit
Weir bashing

Add to these physical definitions the following :

Exploration of one's personality
Exploration of the world about
A means to escape the many people who crowd in upon one
To find remote places
To seek violence almost as an art form, and savour it
To satisfy the Ulysses factor within us
To enjoy, vicariously, the heroism of the 'Cockleshell Heroes'

Which Canoes and Equipment Will Suit My Needs?

The surf ski mentioned on p.25 does not require a spray deck. One sits instead upon an exposed deck, the waves wash across and chill what one sits upon. Knees turn blue on windy days. In the seat pan and feet wells there surges some four to six pints of water. On warm days on sunny surfing beaches this is fine. Short story follows.

In the far West of Wales there is a lifesaving club. Four young lads wished to learn the Eskimo roll. The club captain tried to teach them. Working as he must in the sandy surge of the sea's edge, he found the lads could not accustom themselves to being 'trapped' (their words) in the kayak cockpit with the spray deck on. Rolling success, nil. The club bought a Byde ski with tree. Thighs clenched, the lads rolled at once, or nearly so. They then transferred their new skill and new confidence to kayaks, which they then rolled without problems, without, I may add, a spray deck. What we have here is not an either/or thing, but a new addition to one's battery of resources.

You, the novice, do not know what your needs are, but you can come to recognise them. You don't know which canoe suits the water on which you may fulfil your needs, but you will come to find it. The technical expertise involved in knowing which laminated paddles remain stuck together and which shed their pieces under stress ... all this can be learned the less difficult way : Join a Club!

CHAPTER FIVE

How Do I Get a Canoe?

(All prices quoted in this chapter are at 1973 levels, i.e. before inflation and large increases in the price of oil, the feedstock from which resin is obtained. All prices quoted should be doubled, and in some cases trebled. For example, it now costs £30 for an amateur to build a complete slalom kayak from materials supplied. A good second-hand canoe will cost about £40. (November 1976))

A good sequence is as follows (2 and 3 are interchangeable) :
1. Borrow and use several types;
2. Buy, new or second-hand, depending on cash available;
3. Building, depending on club resources.

Canoe manufacturers have criticised the enthusiasm with which I encourage people to build their own canoes, they argue that it will put them out of business. On the contrary, canoeing business seems now to be booming. One cannot go canoeing without a canoe, and it is unlikely that one will risk a great deal of personal cash on a first-class new canoe unless persuaded that it is a good thing to do. Therefore, become convinced that canoeing is for you by borrowing canoes from your local club, school or youth group, then build your own. Then, becoming dissatisfied with the faults inherent in amateur-built canoes, *buy* a first-class canoe.

Clubs are rarely in a position to buy new commercially built canoes, but can build passably good and useful canoes with moulds and equipment easily purchased.

One may be given an old canoe, or find a framework covered with rotting canvas in some shed. My best advice is, consign it to the flames, and build a new canoe, preferably in G.R.P. Many times people have come to me for advice on how to rebuild an old canvas canoe. The stringers are brittle, the frames cracked and delaminated, the screws pulled loose, and the varnish dry and flaking. Renovation requires skill, care, time and money. The canvas cover for a canoe will cost almost as much as the whole cost of a new G.R.P. canoe.

Second-hand sources are various. Some firms which hire canoes sell their summer fleet each winter when stocking up for the next year. Write to these firms and enquire about second-hand canoes.

Some schools may have an old fleet which they are clearing out. However, it is usual for school groups, which are usually hard up, to run their fleets 'into the ground'. Some canoeing clubs will sell older canoes, and many active canoe clubs, especially slalom types, will have many fairly new canoes available. Some of these are nearly new and first-class. Some are nearly new, but badly damaged, some are insurance write-offs that have been re-assembled from the bits, some last year's models but barely used. Prices vary, and at the time of writing a good second-hand, one-year-old canoe costs about £20–£35.

The Centre of which I am warden has several canoe moulds, and we can build new canoes easily. I prefer to keep the club fleet and the schools fleet no more than two years, thus keeping up quality and style. The second-hand canoes are sold for at least the cost of the materials to replace them, about £15 in our case.

The best thing for the person who wants a canoe but has little idea of what he needs, is to seek the advice of people who do. You cannot really know what you want until you have tried several canoes, watched what can be achieved in them by experienced paddlers, and listened to the opinions of the experienced. Go along to a local club, or to a school with canoes and talk to the person in charge; you will be made welcome and will learn a lot. Buy a copy of the magazine *Canoeing* (see back of book for details), and borrow a copy of *Canoeing in Britain*, the journal of the British Canoe Union (later you will want to join the B.C.U. and you will get your copy free as a member). From these magazines you will be able to see the range and prices of canoes currently available, information which can also be obtained from the catalogues of the manufacturers.

For a detached view of the matter you should write to the

Central Council for Physical Recreation, and ask for a canoeing course at one of their Centres, say Bisham Abbey on the Thames, or Plas Y Brenin in Snowdonia, North Wales, or at Glenmore in Scotland. Here you would use several different types of canoe, and have the opportunity to talk canoeing with the instructors. Other organisations run canoeing courses, such as the Y.H.A. at Lostwithiel in Cornwall, or the Y.M.C.A. Outward Bound does use canoeing as part of its general purpose, but their purpose is not canoeing, and is therefore less reliable in canoeing terms.

The final word on the subject still remains with the canoeists who are organised. You can find them by writing to the British Canoe Union and by asking for details of the regional canoeing courses run by the National Coaches.

This might sound more like a chapter on how to canoe rather than on where to get your canoe; but it is certain that you won't know what you want until you've tried several canoes, and talked with several people, and maybe argued the case on several occasions. Also, you may come in lucky for one of the end-of-season bargains that can be had rather more frequently now than in the past.

Not everyone will be near to a club which can help as ours can, and so my advice then is, buy a kit, either frame, stringer and canvas, or sheet plywood. These kits are very well supplied with everything needed, and are better for one-off jobs.

There are various types of canoe kits. At the time of writing you can get a ply frame, stringer and canvas kit for about £16, but this method requires some skill with woodworking tools, and is long and tedious in comparison with G.R.P. methods. However, it is suitable for one-off boats, even though it requires a lot of care in use.

You can get excellent kits for plywood canoes which are stitched together with nylon ties and then sealed with G.R.P. tape. These are also about £16 per kit, and fairly easy to build, being thoroughly thought out, with the sheets cut to size, all ready for joining up. These boats have the slight disadvantage that the chine design concentrates wear and tear along the chines, thus abrading the G.R.P. seals and leading to seepage, which can usually only be properly cured by re-taping. This is a workshop job, and requires several days to dry out the boat so that the resin will stick to the wood.

A system designed by Bob Vardy an amateur at first, but now a canoe manufacturer (Avoncraft, Redbourn, Hertford-shire) provides a plywood hull and deck with gentle curves. This method is unique, and uses staples fired in by a stapling gun to hold the ply sheets together. A sheet of glass cloth is resined into the inside to hold it all together. This method makes a very strong and lightweight boat, but it requires a mould or form over which the sheets are held for stapling. This method is more suitable for group building projects.

A method which hasn't really caught on, but which has some very good points in its favour is the D.K. method, where a pair of ply sheets are scarfed together to make a sixteen by four sheet, and then an outline and gussets are carefully cut in the sheet. As it is pulled together with wire ties the rather flattened shape of the boat begins to show. After internal stringers have been added and one or two internal frames, then a very presentable boat is the result. Plans are available for this method from the designer Dennis J. Davis. It is light and strong, has no chines, and is suitable for one-off work without a mould.

Incidentally chines, or longitudinal hard edges are not necessarily a bad feature in a canoe. Some sea-going kayaks seem to offer better sea-keeping qualities if they have chines; these seem to 'stiffen' the hull in the water, and constant abrasion of sharp corners is not usually a fault of sea-going boats as it is in river boats.

Finally, the method that gets my vote every time in my particular circumstances is the G.R.P. moulded boat. This requires a workshop designed for this purpose, an organisa-tion suited to turning out these canoes in numbers, and re-latively inexpensive materials. Whilst this method has a low cost per boat factor, it requires skilful organisation, in re-ducing unit costs by making best use of the facilities.

The G.R.P. boat costs about £10 per boat in materials only, but the necessary hand creams, cleaners and so on cost additional money. The moulds, if bought commercially, will be about £65, and so it would cost about £5 per boat if you only built twelve, just for mould cost. However, you can hire moulds about £1.50 per day now, and you can, if you try hard and have skilled direction, build a canoe per day. Adding the cost of going for the mould and returning it, over, say, 100 miles will again bring the mould cost per boat up to about £3.50 if you build three in five days, including travel. If, however, you have your own moulds, and build say fifty boats out of them (after which time the moulds will be ruined, or worn out), then the mould cost per boat becomes much less.

If the manufacturer doesn't mind (and you should ask him for permission first), you can copy the moulds which you originally obtained and which are now wearing out, by building around a suitably prepared 'plug' which is taken from the moulds when they are nearly new. The plug is simply a heavyweight canoe, and can be used as a canoe later if you like. The mould then costs about £15 for the materials.

It may be that you have ideas and want to build your own set of moulds to your own shape. This can be expensive in terms of time, and you must have confidence in your ability to design successfully, in order to avoid expensive mistakes. In this case the plug materials may cost about £12, the mould cost about £15, but the time cost is horrifying, being several hundred hours. This is probably only acceptable if you can sell the rights to copy it, or use it, as in a centre for making many repeat models.

Building a Canoe From the Idea

This sub-section is fairly detailed, and may not be much use to you as a beginner. Even so, it is included so that you may have some understanding of the various processes which go into obtaining the finished canoe on the water. Also, the section is a warning, as I have met several people with more enthusiasm than knowledge who set out to design and build a canoe. But being warned, do not abandon hope. There is no training course anywhere that will tell you how to design a canoe; no technical college that issues certificates in this branch of the sport; but now there is one book which gives the necessary details for some understanding of the subject. It is *Canoe Design and Construction*, published by Pelham in 1975. I wrote it, despite the fact that I have had no training relevant to the job, bar some useful experience, but I am about to write a book called 'Build Your Own Canoe'. It will deal in detail with the various stages necessary in designing and building a new boat in glass reinforced plastic. Canoe design is an art rather than a science, as yet. Some use test tanks for improving sprint craft but I must rely on experience in use.

When I design a boat I rely on three things, the fact that:

1. I've been canoeing since 1957.
2. I've been in many parts of Britain, taken part in most aspects of canoeing sport, have seen most of the types of canoe available, and talked to many really knowledgeable people, some who can design their own boats, too.
3. I have an ability to draw well, or well enough to turn out readable drawings, and an ability to handle woodworking tools, and resin and glass.

The stages of building a new design are as follow:

1. The idea
2. The criticism and sketching
3. The definitive drawings
4. The plug
5. The mould
6. The boat

The 'idea' is based on past experience, present needs, and future probable movements, plus some luck in how the idea is planted. The more new designs you attempt, the more likely you are to be accurate in your most recent work.

Next, one would naturally want to sketch the shape, talk about it with people who know, and generally adjust one's ideas. This stage may last a year or two, I find. Initially it is helpful to make a 1 : 10 scale solid model or two, before detailed drawings, but following general outlines. I use balsa and plaster of Paris for this.

When beginning the drawings I use three sheets of squared paper, about 20 in. by 30 in. and a suitable pencil. Having decided the plan view, I draw that in a scale 1 : 10, also the profile. On another sheet I draw the master section, or cross section at the widest point. A great deal of knowledge goes into selecting this shape, as it affects the whole character of the boat, much more than the outline in plan or profile.

Using now a method which I worked out for myself, I draw the gunwale line in plan, the calculation waterline in plan, and the deck profile and keel line in profile showing the rocker, plus gunwale line showing sheer, and the waterline (which is, of course, straight). These lines are shown full width and height, but are condensed by a factor of five or six for length.

These lines are then measured, using the squared paper, and points are 'taken off' and placed on another sheet of paper to give the sections, usually at one-foot intervals. Given a full set of cross sections, which must all harmonise with each other, a good tracing can then be made, bringing together all the various necessary parts. These are the 1 : 10 scale outline, plus a full set of sections. It is good practice to work out the buoyancy of the immersed part of the canoe, to relate this to the weight of water displaced, and so to construct a graph showing the calculated buoyancy for three waterlines with the draught in inches along the horizontal axis, and the calculated buoyancy up the vertical. If you have a buoyancy of about 180 lb., plus or minus 20 lb. at a four-inch draught, then the boat is about right for a solo.

The actual drawing takes me about six hours, complete with calculations. At this point I may wait several weeks in order to show the drawings to various people who can understand and criticise. Then I start to build the plug. There are so many ways in which this can be done, but possibly the best so far is to make a spine of 3 in. by 3 in. planed and straight timber, full length. On to this are slotted the frame shapes cut from blockboard according to tracings taken from the drawings, and allowing for the skin thickness of the plug. This skeleton is clad with $1\frac{1}{2}$ mm. ply sheets stapled into position. I have used heavy cardboard from the many packing cases given away by supermarkets, but that buckles too easily.

The carcass is then skinned with at least two layers of $1\frac{1}{2}$

ounce chopped strand mat. When this has hardened and been tidied up it is possible to fill it, using car body filler paste. I use a sixteen-pound tin per boat, costing about £3. The hardened filler is shaped by using a heavy sanding disc initially, with further filling and levelling with a suitable spreader. It is then filed with car body files to bring it to a good profile without ripples. You can see a number of boats today, including some of my earlier ones, with distinct rippling of the surface, although highly polished. This means that the plug builder is a patient man, but lacks knowledge of the proper techniques.

The rough finished plug is painted with four coats of surface primer, half an hour between coats, and allowed to dry for twenty-four hours. This is then cut down with 60, 80 and 180 grade wet and dry rubbing paper. It then receives two more coats of primer, and is rubbed down with 180 and then 360 grade paper. Finally it receives two more coats of special resin, the last one being rubbed down with 360, then 600 grade paper.

The whole is then cut down by a 5 in. calico polishing mop on an electric drill with medium and then coarse cutting paste (as used in car body work, and quite cheap). Then I use an American cutting down paste (Formula 'C'), incorporating a mould glaze, for polishing. This now should give a glossy plug surface without ripples and blemishes. At this point the plug is very vulnerable and needs great care in handling. It should then receive at the very least three coats of the proper polish; better still, five coats of polish with at least six hours between each coat of polish, followed by the application of a release agent before casting commences.

At this point there is a complete hull and deck shape, weight about one hundredweight, with the cockpit rim hole in its proper place. I often 'cheat' here by grafting on a well-used and trusted cockpit rim shape from another canoe. It saves on having to alter spray deck shapes. The flanges for the mould must now be attached, and this is done in hardboard, stiffened with 2 in. by 1 in. battens on the edges, the whole attached by bent slips of alloy fixed by self-tapping screws and pop rivets, direct to the plug, with the flange edge running along where the joint on the canoe is required. The first half of the mould is cast, usually the deck first, using three layers of 1½-ounce glass mat. The laminates set, then the whole is turned over and the fence for the flange stripped off. Polish and release agent is applied, and the other half of the mould is laminated up to the new flange as cast on the first half of the mould.

The moulds are left to set for a day or two, then separated from the plug, which is then either thrown away, or put away just in case, and thrown away a year or two later. The moulds are then corrected, any slight blemishes rubbed out, and the cutting down and polishing process is repeated. Then you can cast your first boat.

Please remember, if all this sounds off-putting, that I, too, was a complete ignoramus in these matters in 1959. Don't be put off. If you are going to design boats, you *will* design boats, and nobody will stop you. It just takes a great deal of effort, but the satisfaction is in direct ratio with the amount of work put in. A rough guess at the number of people designing canoes in Britain now would be about five professionals, and about ten amateurs. There is a great deal of room for improvement.

To summarise, if you want to get a canoe :

1. Get skilled advice.
2. Try out several designs of boat and several types.
3. Decide what you want.
4. Buy second-hand, or build through a club.
5. Use it for a season.
6. Then, either give up canoeing, and sell the equipment you have, or improve your equipment in the light of knowledge gained in the first season.

(*N.B. Chapter 8 will give more details on how to build a canoe in glass-reinforced plastic*)

CHAPTER SIX

Where Can I Use My Canoe?

In Britain almost all land is the property of someone. Between high water mark and low water mark there is land which usually belongs to the Crown. However, an irate landowner may have you off his private beach at low tide and claim, possibly wrongly, that that piece of 'land' is his. If you are on the sea or estuary you may still be asked to leave that area, for example if a sea fishing contest is in progress, or maybe anglers are heaving two-pound lead weights off a pier end into the sea, and the lines are barbed with hooks in profusion.

Sometimes it does not do to argue the point. There was once a gun battle off a pier end in the North Sea between sea anglers using lead weights with great accuracy and outraged canoeists using an air gun with more fury than accuracy, especially as the 'gun platform' was bobbing about like a cork. And I was once on a river passing heavily wooded banks and a twelve bore boomed among the bushes and leaves ripped from the tree a mere six feet overhead. We had no specific permission to be there, and we couldn't identify the gunner, so we left, fairly smartly!

Angry disputes are few, thank goodness, but pressure on available waters is increasing rapidly and some rivers which were available to canoeists now have 'Canoeing Forbidden' notices nailed to trees, above notices stating 'Blank Angling Club – Strictly Private. No Licences'. Water skiers want their bit of water, sailors theirs, and so on. There is already a need for separating groups from each other either by time or

49

distance. Even anglers can interfere with each others needs for fishing waters, and with estimated club memberships of something like 3 million in Britain, compared with the 6,000 canoeists who are club members, anglers are obviously going to have to fit in with each other, never mind all the other groups laying claim to the use of a water.

Some people are quite happy to see canoeists using their waters, but they do like first to be asked. A peer of the realm once caught me and my two companions on a piece of river for which we did not have permission. Frankly, we didn't know we needed permission, but that is a long time ago. He called us over, hauled us over the coals, then relented and asked us to help him to launch a particularly heavy and tarry salmon boat. We did, and he then remarked that it really did give him pleasure to see young men shooting the rapids on his stretch. We parted on good terms.

Another man, a guardian on the river Tweed, said that there were over three hundred landowners on the hundred miles we had done to that place, and that to get permission from each of them, while theoretically correct was clearly impracticable, and maybe impossible, as some lived in Australia and were difficult to contact. But, in future, if we phoned him he would let us know who was using the river for game fishing, and where they would be, and in general advise us of the propriety of using a given section.

Well, these problems are not new to canoeists and to others who know of rivers and their uses. Recently the landowners, the angling interests and the canoeists have met under the wing of the National Sports Council in an attempt to solve the problems, and some form of organisation seems to be developing. It depends on registration of canoes and of canoeists, with clear registration marks on canoes; on agreement between groups as to which rivers can be used, and when; and on the National Sports Council being powerful enough to give effect to the proposals. Unless this happens we have anarchy, and violence is the likely result of that. Clearly, regulations without sanctions are powerless, as appeals to good behaviour will always fail with a very small but significant section of any community. How to 'police'

a river and identify canoes without marks, and then successfully take a case to court where some infringement of use for
that river has been detected baffles me. I have a vivid impression of some energetic bailiff leaping madly through briar
thickets, hurtling wildly over riverside bluffs, and swimming
like a seal to get near enough to a fast-moving canoe on a
rugged piece of river, surrounded by cheering anglers. I guess
it would beat fishing for sport!

But rely upon it, some way of avoiding clashes of interest
must be found, and about twenty years ago would have been
just in time.

One of the questions is, do I favour registration? Well,
no. But the alternatives which appear in this tight little island
of ours are rather too horrible to contemplate. So, accepting
registration and reasonable behaviour by all concerned as
being the lesser of the evils offered, then I heartily support it.

Canoeists are, it seems, loners by nature, tending to asocial
habits, if not actual anti-social behaviour. I suppose all sports
have their rough characters, and so does canoeing. Those who
are reasonable people are not those to cause trouble anyway,
and so registration for them is no difficulty. But the person
who wants to get away from it all will still do so, and registration to that one is likely to be anathema. My personal
attitude at present is to seek out the lonely places, and these
are usually off our coasts. In the sunny car park on the cliff
top hundreds of people sit picnicking, in bright sunlight,
with ice cream vans, shops selling knick-knacks and funny
hats, all our bright fun-giving commercialism. Four hundred
feet away, measured vertically, in dark caverns and green
translucent water, with a miner's helmet lamp, the sea cave
canoeist floats in a lost realm, unknown to all but a very few
in the history of the world.

In contrast, I have spent many more summer days happily
by the slipway by the Centre which I run, swimming, practising rolling, and generally frolicking in the warm waters of
the Isis or Thames. (A forty-year-old man, thirteen stone,
frolicking, is a powerful sight to see!) Many score of people
come to the place, and dozens will be playing about there,
with rubber tyres and small canoes and a generally happy air.

In winter time we make for the workshop and the swimming pool, and we either make canoes ready for next summer, or we learn to handle the tiny baths boats, rolling, support strokes, and the whole range of full-size strokes ready for next year. The advantage of a bath is that the water is warm, clear and clean, and if the drain hole is not too large one cannot lose one's charges down the drain.

FREEDOM TO USE THE WATER

Generally the situation is as follows, regarding freedom to use the water.

Navigable rivers. There is usually a conservancy board, as on the Thames, to which one pays a licence fee for putting a canoe on the water.

First-class fishing rivers (Game fish, i.e., salmon). These are usually tied up tight in England and Wales, with bailiffs to watch over them, but some, like the Wye and the Severn, have old-established rights of way, and so some canoeing is possible on them. In Scotland these rivers are usually more accessible to canoeists, but as yet fewer canoeists wish to use them. As the numbers increase, restrictions will be imposed, but a case on the Spey allowed a canoeing centre to use the Spey, subject to thoughtful behaviour.

Non-game-fishing rivers. These are often available to canoeists, especially if in their lower reaches the water is heavily contaminated by industrial effluents. However, some such rivers are actually becoming less polluted, and so some fish are running up the rivers. In addition to this, the higher reaches can be stocked with coarse fish, and some angling groups are paying a great deal of money to secure for themselves the right to fish in future, and so they will not take kindly to canoeists passing as freely as they did, say, ten years previously.

Fishing off-season. Angling off-seasons vary with the species of fish and position of the water. The salmon off-season is from October 1st to January 25th; the trout off-season is from October 1st to the last day of February, and the coarse fishing off-season from March 15th to June 15th. But this is a general guide only for game fishing. Coarse fishing and sea fishing each have their own seasons. Salmon netting, i.e., on the Towy, is not the same season as the rod and fly man's season.

Flood. It is rarely possible for anglers to succeed in fishing when rivers are thundering along with muddy brown water well above normal, so these are the times when the experienced canoeist is in his element.

Canals. These are run by the Inland Waterways Board, and they charge quite heavy fees for the licences which they issue.

Harbours. Some harbours, such as Langstone, near Portsmouth, may attempt to obtain fees from canoeists passing across the harbour. On one occasion a harbour launch came alongside a group and demanded money. None was handed over as they were not carrying more than the cost of a phone call, but they gave the address of the Centre from which they had come. Nothing more was heard of it. Mind, if you launch from the harbour it seems reasonable to pay a reasonable launching fee for the privilege of using private land for the purpose.

Estuaries. That is, the lower reaches of rivers, which are subject to tidal ebb and flow. The highest point of the tidal influence is marked on Ordnance survey maps. I once tried to argue that point with a very, very irate Welshman on the Conway Estuary, but he would have none of it. These banks were his master's land, and his master's fishing was being spoiled by the canoeists of whom I was in charge. We kept the argument going as politely as possible until we reached our intended pull-out point, and then asked if we could come ashore? He at once refused, and demanded that we leave the water forthwith. Lacking wings, as I pointed out, we now found ourselves in an impossible situation. We did get away in due course, but it did upset that man, and I don't like to see people upset on my account. I fear if I had produced my one-inch O.S. map that he would have produced a Welsh Dragon to devour it by fire!

The Sea. Usually available, but if you launch at Kimmeridge Bay in Dorset, for example, and, as you paddle westwards, admire the pretty red flags and the charming soldiery shouting encouragement from the low cliffs, it should come as no surprise to be ordered off the water by a young man in a high-speed patrol launch which has come up from nowhere, lest you be selected by the computer as the next gunner's waterborne target. And close under the cliffs at Whitburn in Durham, it is possible, or it was some years ago, to listen carefully and hear buzzing, as of bees, and note the little fountains of spray a few score yards seawards. Being downrange of the butts as .303s were firing is a little dangerous. However, by keeping well under the cliffs we used their shelter as cover. A man in uniform on the cliffs was quite angry about it, but we couldn't hear what he was saying for the thunder of the breaking waves a few yards away.

Islands. Someone once counted the islands in Britain, and measured the length of the coastline, and in both cases it amounts to far more than you possibly could imagine. However, if you attempt to land on Inner Farne during the summer, off Northumberland, then a man with a cash bag will come along and ask you for money – 35 new pence, I think it was, in 1972. Also, most of those islands are protected by the National Trust, and nesting sites on the ground could be ruined by people who did not know what they were doing Another island off Scotland was the site of wartime experiments in bacteriological warfare, and it seems that now the very soil is deadly with dormant bugs, ready to seek out and savage the canoeist who ignores the many notices to keep off. However, most islands are safe, and one I know of, and wouldn't dream of saying where it is, is about one acre in size and should sink with the weight of luscious brambles on it in September. It's only half a mile from shore – an easy ten minutes' paddle.

Beaches. Surfing in canoes is great fun, but so is swimming in the surf, and riding boards, and so on. A busy afternoon in, say Cornwall, the beach can be very crowded, and a canoeist coming in through the break, riding a ten-foot wave is caught by the toppling waterfall off the crest and hurled forward, unstoppable for many yards. It is too easy to smash into some swimmer or another canoeist, and, apart from overcrowding, this shows lack of consideration for other people. Other beaches are safe and allow more scope for canoeing; the break of the wave is progressive, and the release of energy in the wave as it meets the shallower water is gentle and progressive, too. Some beaches are 'dumper' beaches, and all the great energy of the wave is released in a few feet with smashing impact. One can be caught between the hammer of the wave crest falling on to the anvil of the steep beach. And beaches can also have dangerous tide rips and undertow.

Lochs and Lakes. Should you go to the Holy Loch and launch your canoe by Dunoon, then do so, and enjoy your calm-water paddle. But remember the protest marches and sit-ins when the American Navy came there with Polaris atomic submarines, and look at the depot ship across the loch, and don't paddle near it. Get within about four hundred yards and a swift speed boat will sweep out, and turn you back. It's tidal water, and it's British, but I wouldn't go there, no fear!

Most lakes are beautiful, and the Lake District spectacularly so. There are many launching spots on Ullswater with no access charge, but look out for the wind tearing down from the high crags. There is little warning, just a rising breeze turning rapidly to a force six or even higher wind, gusty, uncertain in direction, and very violent. Whilst a canoe could possibly ride waves, as a seagull does, that would smash a larger ship by breaking its back, or by broaching and flooding it, I would not wish to put that theory to the test.

Some of the most scenically satisfying canoeing can be had on lakes. Derwentwater is another beautiful lake, but, should you go down the river linking it with Bassenthwaite, remember that the second lake is mostly on a private estate, and that the river between is heavily populated by fishing interests which are not very happy about canoeists using that river. A centre for outdoor education on that river has to watch carefully what canoeists do there in case it affects their rights.

Swimming Baths. These are very much more open to the idea that indoor waters can reasonably be used by people in canoes. Canoe polo and training can take place there in relative warmth. The usual source of trouble there is filters blocked with bits of canoe, especially polystyrene foam fragments from the buoyancy blocks in the canoes. Allegations of tiles cracked by fast travelling canoes have been made, and I would never use a metal tipped paddle in a bath, in case of scratching tiles or even tearing plastic liners, never mind potential injury.

Park pools. Parks and Gardens Departments in many councils are developing the idea of making parks and gardens places for recreation in an active sense instead of for passive admiration of beautiful walks, floral arrangements, and open places. The new city of Milton Keynes long ago planned waterways as an integral part of its provision in years to come for recreation in the City. But, a word of warning, do keep the novice canoeists away from the rowing people! They do so like to thunder along in reverse, as it were, concentrating on the shoulders of the man in front (or should that read 'behind'?), and the typical British lunacy of putting cox where he can't see where he is going for all the great big men in front of him makes the passage of one of these three-quarter-ton boats, travelling at upwards of ten m.p.h. and carving out a swathe, blade tip to blade tip of something like twenty-two feet, a hazardous business for other water users if they happen to be in its track. I admire rowing, but from the safety of the bank, please. It's a sixty-foot-long wooden skewer for canoeist kebabs!

If you want my opinion, then I would put it as follows. I enjoy canoeing when it is warm, and I am warm. I don't like travelling on our roads now, but I will if I must. Given a place to practise on, and some wild places to which I may go and where no one is there to argue in an aggressive manner about it – a remote wild place – then I am satisfied. But I fear that encouraging people to take up canoeing with the enthusiasm which I have, is counter-productive. All these lovely remote places will become the haunt of other canoeists, and so we search further and further away for our sense of wonder and joy in nature.

However, one thing gives me hope.

Britain is still a big, big place, with so many islands that you can't visit them all, and a coastline so great that even a round-Britain paddler in 1972 went from headland to headland, and cut through a canal to miss the furthest headlands and tide races. When Britain is too circumscribed with necessary restrictions on freedom of movement then there will be the rest of the world. New Zealand marks out a track each side of every one of its rivers, and for a certain distance inland from its shores, and these areas are vast and they belong to the nation, and no one may say 'this is my land, keep off!' France has rivers which are accessible to all, and the Scandinavian countries have great rivers, wild and free, and even bigger mosquitoes, which are wilder and freer with their bites, or so I am told.

Where can I use my canoe? I'd rather put that, where can I enjoy my canoe? There's a pleasure in making them, and in using them on water and even on land. But one thing is certain, if you want to savour canoeing at its best you must put it on some transport and take it where the water is, and that means a car and time and money. It's no accident that some ace canoeists could be good rally drivers if they wished.

CHAPTER SEVEN

When Should One Learn?

People frequently come to me during the summer, as I stand by the river, or more often now in the workshop, and ask that their child receive instruction in canoeing at Riverside. Very often these children are about ten years old. Have you ever seen a child of ten, about five foot, give or take a foot or two, in a lifejacket made for an adult? Note the droopy spray deck which slips slackly over skinny hips, the enormous paddle like a lance, the canoe that he cannot carry alone, and when in it finds it tight about the armpits? I've seen 'em, and despite all this outsize equipment they stagger bravely to the water, a light in their eyes, willingness in every move. It is my opinion that at present canoes dictate who uses them and that the nature of the canoes available has a definite effect on the type of people who find them interesting. There is a growing body of younger people who want to get into canoes for fun, just pottering about on a pool, with supervision near. They have a take-it-or-leave-it attitude, and are uncommitted.

These demands on canoeing provision are rather different from those of the man, say, who dearly needs to escape his normal life and who needs to get near to raw nature, from which his car, his house, his office and the pavements insulate him. This man is often over thirty, he is experienced on the water, and seeks far horizons. They are not many, but now and again they turn up.

There is a teacher in Staffordshire, who helped me by criticising my first book, *Living Canoeing*. He had been canoeing for years before I met him, and had enjoyed pottering about on beautiful surroundings, like the Mawddach Estuary in North Wales, in a tubby double canoe. What I like to call inexpensive drifting. We met, and we canoed together, and we did some canoeing in that two years, the like of which I've never bettered.

We went out on a frightful tide race, explored sea cliffs, and made canoes and talked to people and set others off on the canoeing adventure, children and adults. He, despite his protestations that he never would, learned to roll, and could teach others to roll quite effortlessly. He was in his middle forties when I met him and had a war injury which made his back a bit stiff. Last I heard from him, he was up in the north of Scotland with bicycle, canoes, and tent.

There was another man, one of the social crowd which enjoyed camping and canoeing at Beadnell in Northumberland. I have a vivid impression of him, fully clothed, taking a canoe out for a little potter along the beach and falling in. He trudged wetly through the camp site, with such a funny look on his face, and he hung up his clothes to dry, and people around said, 'come and see!' And we did and at one end of his clothes line were seven or eight treasury notes pinned up to dry. He was a man nearer forty than thirty when the urge to go canoeing took him.

None the less, is the growing crowd of young people in the middle teens, from fourteen to eighteen, who want very much to find something, somebody, maybe themselves. It doesn't matter whether its canoeing or flower arranging, if it interests them then they should have the chance to try it, and no artificial barriers such as canoe size or weight, timetable at school, or some rather outdated concept of loyalty to the club or group, or a City boundary, or whatever should prevent them from taking up canoeing and leaving it when they have had enough. Some never have enough, and some don't like it ever, but at least they've had the opportunity.

If you're skinny, fourteen, suffering from poliomyelitis in one leg, using a clapped-out, borrowed canvas canoe on a grubby dock in a big manufacturing city in the north, don't be put off; the description I've just given is of a boy who became a member of the British Slalom Team.

Those are the thoughts that the word 'when' brings to me. But there is a also definite 'when' related to the year, and I reckon on a closed season from mid-October to early April. It's too cold during that time for most youngsters to start canoeing, and believe me I'd far rather be in the workshop in the sweet sickening reek of synthetic resin fumes (you get to like them) building canoes on the principle that if I make them, they'll break them, so I'd better start right away. During winter, if some local club runs a canoeing course in the baths, go there and start the easy way, and learn to roll; its the best self-rescue method known yet, and takes two seconds compared with up to two minutes for a quick rescue by others. If anything goes wrong you just pop up again. 'Ye Gods! Self righting canoes!' as someone once said.

There is a fair bit of psychology in choosing the time and place and your companions to begin canoeing. If it's a fine warm day, in early summer, and the water is warmish after, say, a week of strong sun, say early June, then go on the river. The sea is warmest with a gentle on-shore breeze, about late August or early September on the west coast somewhere; or on the shores of a big shallow area like Cardigan Bay, towards the end of the day after the sun has warmed up many square miles of sea by reflection from the shallow sandy bottom. Off Abersoch, on an ebbing tide in the evening after such a day, the water is like that in an indoor heated swimming pool. Mind, we had porpoises there too, and you don't find them in a pool. Give yourself a good experience to begin with. Don't, as you value the good name of the sport, be cajoled into putting one tentative foot into a cold, wet, muddy canoe on a bitter afternoon in November as the wind tears the dying leaves from the trees, and the grey gloom pervades everything including the soul. In those circumstances, don't bother.

My critics have asked me to be specific about the age ranges that I think should normally be included in the question 'when'. So I would suggest :

Age six to twelve, with parental supervision.

Age twelve to eighteen, with responsible supervision.
Eighteen plus? Any time you want to!

Finally, I would not refuse to accept a non-swimmer, but I would insist on knowing this, and I would not accept that person unless I could give almost undivided attention. Later I would expect the canoeing to give a good reason for wanting to learn to swim.

Since this book was written, the previous para has caused about as much comment as the rest of the book put together. I stand by what I state, that I will encourage a non-swimmer to learn to canoe provided that I know who he is, that I can devote my entire attention to him, and that it is understood that he never canoes without skilled supervision until he learns to swim well. Down by the pool side at Atlantic College, the summer after this book was first published, a stranger talked to me. He was tall, and an excellent swimmer. He teaches swimming. He mentioned that he had just read a book on canoeing and that the writer had encouraged non-swimmers to go canoeing. He then lead off about this, and went on at some length. I didn't tell him then who had written the book, but later we met again and he was very embarrassed. He still sticks to his guns, and I to mine. Interestingly he is now a Senior Instructor within the British Canoe Union Coaching Scheme.

CHAPTER EIGHT

Canoe Building and the Workshop

There are many ways of building canoes, and they are, briefly, as follows:

1. Carved from solid. Wood, e.g. Maori war canoe, sixty paddlers. Foam plastic. Not yet tried commercially.
2. Framework. Ply frame, stringers, and canvas, Ultra-thin G.R.P. laminate supported by carbon fibre.
3. Planked hull. Clinker built, e.g. Rob Roy, Rushton. Shaped and stitched ply sheets. Kayel method.
4. Stressed skin. G.R.P. (Glass re-inforced plastic) Cold or hot moulded veneer strip or sheet. Ply-glass laminate composites. Vardy, D.K. method.

This chapter will deal with construction in G.R.P., but if you want to know more about the other methods, you should consult the following:

Framework: Canoes and Canoeing by Percy Blandford, Lutterworth Press. (And many other books) Note. Details of the carbon fibre re-inforcement of G.R.P. laminates are mostly in various parts of technical articles, Hailed as a technological marvel, which it is, it was quickly found that its cost was prohibitive, and the method of use gives rise to stress concentration and cracking of the surrounding laminates.

Kayel planked method: Technical information and drawings from 'Ottersports', Ash Street, Northampton.

Vardy method: Bob Vardy, Avoncraft, Burrowfield, Welwyn Garden City, Herts, AL7 4SP.

Cold moulding: Veneers *Complete Amateur Boat Builder* by

Michael Verney, published by John Murray.

G.R.P. methods: Booklets published by firms in the business, e.g. Strand Glass, Trylon, Streamlyte.

A beautifully moulded, polished, brightly coloured kayak or canoe is fine sight on the water, but in order to bring it to that finished condition the following stages have to be passed:

1. Experience of canoes in use, say 10 years.
2. Design and drawing, 10 hours.
3. Construction of pattern or plug, 20 hours.
4. Polishing and finishing plug, 100 hours.
5. Making mould, 20 hours.
6. Making boat, 10 hours.

Most amateur boat builders will start at stage six, and make a few boats, and that will be enough. It is this stage that this chapter will describe in a little detail. A few of these people will copy a set of moulds, stage five. Schoolteachers and scout leaders and so on will find that having their own set of moulds is useful if they intend to have a fleet of canoes ready for use, say ten or more.

A few people will be going through stage one with some enthusiasm and will find that whatever it is they have, it won't do. So alterations to existing designs are made, and new ideas pop up, and soon one realises that the only possible way to make a good boat as you want it is to design it. The first attempt at design takes weeks, not hours, but it is true to state that the actual skilled work of putting lines on paper when you know what you are doing is not very time-consuming; it is, however, based on the confidence of years of use of canoes.

G.R.P. MATERIALS

Chopped strand glass mat. This is usually 36 inches wide, and in rolls about 70 yards long. It is measured for weight in ounces per square foot, or now, in grams per square metre. New rolls will be produced in metre widths when Britain goes metric. The equivalents will then be, 1½ ounce glass mat becomes 450 gsm glass mat. The quality of the mat is generally what used to be known as 'E' type, and is sold as first or second quality. First quality should be perfect. Second quality may have 'bird's nests' in it – lumps of fluffy strands that make a lump in the laminate, and are slow, or impossible, to wet out. These should be plucked out at the start when they become visible, and a little mat, about the size of the palm of your hand, laid over to cover the hole. Also, second quality mat may be tapered edge to edge, perhaps 300 gsm at one edge and 600 gsm at the other and 450 gsm, the nominal size, in the middle.

Woven rovings. Sometimes called glass cloth. If it is tightly woven, aircraft-quality material, it is so difficult to handle that I would never advocate it for amateur work. It is better to go for the cheaper, loosely woven rovings. This material is measured in ounces per square yard, and 9 oz. woven rovings is the same as 300 gsm woven rovings.

Glass is impregnated, both as cloth and mat, with a binding agent which accepts resin when 'wetted out' (i.e., the resin has thoroughly soaked into the glass mat). As there are nearly 200 different resins, each for a specific purpose, some glass and its binder is more suited to some resin than others. Most resins are polyesters, but epoxy resins require a different binder on the glass. You should check that the materials are compatible.

Gelcoat resin. This is thixotropic, i.e. stays where it is put. It provides the surface for the boat, and is the first layer that goes into the mould.

Laminating resin. This is much thinner, although it has more or less thickener in it. Some resins run like water and are a bit too thin for canoe construction, allowing pinholing and thus seepage in the finished boat. A general-purpose resin as sold by the canoeing suppliers is quite satisfactory. Some resins require an accelerator or promoter to speed up the reaction with the catalyst. This is added when the resin is poured out for use. Nowadays, most amateurs will prefer pre-accelerated resins which are designated by the suffix 'PA'. They may have prefixes, i.e., GL for gelcoat, AP for all-purpose, and so on. The supplier will advise you as to what to use.

The catalyst. An organic peroxide, it supports combustion

in an explosive way, so don't have flame near it. It reacts with the resin and sets up molecular linking which renders the resin solid in about an hour, when it is said to be 'green'. Assuming that the ambient temperature is about 20°C., after about four hours the resin becomes fairly hard, and after twenty-four hours very hard, but the full completion of the linking is not achieved until maybe six weeks have passed. Within this time the typical sweetish smell of setting resin is noticeable. As the resin is reaching the green stage, it gives off heat, and about one pound weight of fast-setting resin in a small pot can give off thick fumes, and crackle and fizz. Such smoking pots should be put outside to cool off.

Cleaner. Many people use acetone, or mixtures including acetone. This is highly inflammable, and my own workshop was seared with flame after three pints of this stuff caught fire, and one youth had his leg badly scorched, with first degree burns from ankle to knee. Never smoke in a G.R.P. workshop, have clear 'NO SMOKING' notices on show and supplementary notices about the other dangers that resins, etc, offer should also be displayed. Another way to clean brushes is to use a powerful detergent, but this must be selected with care. Hot water and soap also assist in cleaning the brushes. By the way, it is not sufficient simply to drop the resin-soaked brush into the solvent, or put it under water, because resin will set anyway anywhere. Time, tide, and setting resin wait for no man. And a final point is that acetone vapour, like petrol, can form an explosive mixture with air at a critical proportion.

Barrier Creams. These are sold by the suppliers, and whilst not essential, should be used especially by young people with skin which has not yet been hardened to work. The cream washes off with warm water and soap after use.

Polish. Provided that it is suitable for resin work, almost any kind will do. A beeswax base is necessary, and the very good quality polishes are imported from U.S.A. and cost about £2.50 for a 12 oz. tin. I use Meguire's 'Mirrorglaze' or Formula 'C', but I am told that Simoniz is as good, and costs much less here. If it is a liquid polish it is not likely to be suitable. Follow the mould supplier's advice on mould polishing.

TOOLS

Brushes. I buy these a dozen at a time, 2 in. laminating brushes with white bristles. The material suppliers also offer these. They are very easily spoiled and it is too easy simply to put one down out of sight, and to forget about it. Half an hour later it is set hard and cannot be recovered. Mind, I have occasionally found one just going off, with the resin all rubbery, and by banging it with a hammer on a hard surface the resin has crumbled away, thus allowing normal cleaning to take place.

Roller. There are several different types. I use a cheap woollen surfaced roller as sold by Woolworths, the 'Handi-rolla'. A better quality mohair roller from the suppliers will cost very much more, but it does a better job. If you are used to this work, I'd advise a mohair roller, but *not* if inexperienced people are likely to use it, as replacement is expensive. Another roller I use is about 5 in. long, 1 in. diameter, and is simply a handle with an alloy rod with ribs turned on it every quarter of an inch. The last roller is a 2 in. wide, 2 in. diameter paddle roller, with the vanes in line with the axis. You may also make some special rollers for various odd jobs as you come to know what you want.

In addition, there are several other tools which are useful:

6 in. screwdriver.

A pallette knife or putty knife.

An old bread knife for stirring.

Two Stanley trimming knives.

A coping saw.

Rasps, or car body files. 2 or 3.

A 3 ft. straight edge. I use a piece of strip alloy, $1\frac{1}{2}$ in. by $\frac{1}{8}$ in.

A pad saw with hacksaw blade.

A two-speed electric drill, with sanders, drills and polishing mop

Two bricklayer's bolsters.

A 2 K.W. fan heater.

A wetting out board, 2 ft. by 6 in., alloy sheet, or ply, or cardboard.

Three or four one-gallon polythene jars, with the tops cut off.

Some cleaning cloths.

Two pairs of trestles to stand the moulds on.

A working area on a bench or table, covered with hardboard, 2 ft. by 4 ft.

A glass cutting table, hardboard surface, 8 ft. by 3 ft. 6 in.

Some polythene sheeting, e.g. (the wrapper the roll of glass comes in).

Canoe Weight

The finished weight of the canoe has a great deal to do with all the considerations. Given it is a solo kayak, then the weight should be roughly as follows:

Ultra lightweight. 18 lb. to 25 lb. Only top-class canoe manufacturers can get down to this weight. Such a boat may last for half a dozen events only.

Lightweight. 25 lb. to 30 lb. Most club members in slalom would use this weight of boat.

Medium lightweight. 30 lb. to 35 lb. This is the weight I build to. This type of boat in a busy riverside centre will last about two seasons.

Heavyweight. 35 lb. to 45 lb. Good for durability but difficult to carry and manoeuvre. Should last five years.

Since being warden of Riverside my attitude to canoes has changed. I would once expect canoes to be heavy and durable. Now I recognise that the person beginning canoeing has different criteria:

1. The canoe is seen. It must be colourful, shiny, and a pleasing shape.

2. The canoe is carried to the water. It must be well balanced and light.

3. The canoe is used. It must handle well for the beginner.

Building Sequence

A solo kayak has several well defined stages in its construction. These are as follows:

minutes.

1. Polish moulds, hull, deck, seat, hull stiffener.   30
2. Cut glass mat and cloth, hull, deck, seat, stiffener.   20
3. Apply gelcoat. Hull deck, cockpit.   20
4. Laminate stiffener.   10
5. Laminate hull.   60
6. Laminate deck.   60
7. Trim stiffener and laminate in place.   10
8. Take a break.   30
9. Trim deck and hull, bolt together.   20
10. Lay in one side joint, end to end.   20
11. Laminate seat.   40
12. Join other side of deck-hull joint.   20
13. Insert end blocks.   10
14. Cut buoyancy blocks.   20
15. Trim seat.   10
16. Take a break.   60
17. Unbolt moulds, take out cast hull and deck.   20
18. Trim casting flash.   10
19. Fit seat to deck hole.   20
20. Fix buoyancy blocks.   10
21. Sling boat, clamp cockpit in place.   20
22. Fix cockpit joint.   20
23. Take a break.   30
24. Fix seat stabilisers.   20
25. Drill end holes.   20
26. Fix one trim stripe.   20
27. Take a break.   30
28. Fix other trim stripe.   20
29. Fit end loops or toggles.   20
30. Go round cockpit with coarse sandpaper to remove all rough edges still left.   10

Total time; about 12 hours.

This assumes skilled work. If not skilled, allow 50 per cent extra for safety margin on time and materials. Longer breaks may be taken between the following stages: 3 and 4; 9 and 10; and 15 and 17.

After stage 17 the job may be left at almost any point. But it is better to reach stage 16 at one go, where possible.

68

MATERIALS : QUANTITIES

This relates to building a K.W. 7 as a semi-lightweight, with one lamination of 10 oz. cloth, one lamination of $1\frac{1}{2}$ oz. mat in the hull, one lamination of $1\frac{1}{2}$ oz. mat over deck, with local cloth stiffening around cockpit.

Hull: Gelcoat, $1\frac{3}{4}$ lb. 12 lb. laminating resin.

Deck: Gelcoat, $1\frac{1}{4}$ lb., 8 lb. laminating resin.

Cockpit: Gelcoat, $\frac{1}{8}$ lb., 2 lb. laminating resin.

Joint takes $1\frac{1}{4}$ lb. of laminating resin to each side.

Total glass weight, Mat, 7 lb., cloth, $3\frac{1}{4}$ lb.

Allowing for waste, etc., this gives a total weight about 30 lb.

CLEANLINESS

For good workmanship the following rules are essential :

1. Never mix resin on the glass bench.
2. Keep the colour pastes well away from the glass bench.
3. Mix resin on a hardboard working surface, which can be burned eventually when thoroughly contaminated with wodges of gooey resin.
4. Clean brushes and rollers at least once an hour when working.
5. Laminate the seat at one go. If you use two mixes of resin there will be difficulties in trimming it.
6. Trim all cast edges with a knife when 'green'; never allow to harden, as cutting with a coping saw later is very tedious.
7. Work clean. If anyone has messy hands, when he picks up a pot of resin, or a knife or a roller or brush, the mess will transfer to that handle. This well then be picked up by someone with hitherto clean hands, and he will then become messy. Be ruthless with messy workers, make them clean up at once.
8. Colour paste on the bottom of a pot, transferred there from a finger, is unnoticed. The person puts the pot down, and picks up glass. The tiny spot of pigment, often black, is unnoticed. But as soon as the laminating resin gets at it, it spreads over a large area of the mould and cast, staining the job.
9. Little bits of rubbish can drop into the job. If glass is

laid over these bits, the glass is 'propped' and cannot lie in place. An air bubble like a ring forms around the rubbish, and a circle of delamination is found.

10. *Therefore,* work clean. Keep the pots clean. Wash down the catalyst bottle with solvent. Wipe your hands often.

11. Clean the brushes and rollers. Especially when the brushes appear to be clean, you can bet they're not. Take a clean piece of cloth, soak it with solvent, then rub the apparently clean bristles of the brush on to it, very firmly. Then it will be clean.

12. Count your brushes and rollers before you start, and check again during work and at the end of it.

COPING WITH DISASTER

One recurrent disaster is the result of forgetting to put the catalyst into the resin mix. The resin simply does not set. The cost of the gelcoat for a complete canoe is about £1.00.

The average novice G.R.P. canoe builder will manage occasionally to forget this vital operation, and the blight falls on experienced builders too. Therefore, to avoid wasting the material by wiping it all out of the moulds, a messy and tedious business, try the following :

Pour out about an eighth of a pint of brush cleaner (acetone). Mix in about 100 ml. of catalyst.

Brush lightly all over the unset resin.

The cleaner helps the catalyst to spread, and then dries out.

The remaining catalyst leaches into the unset resin, thus activating it, and causing it to set.

If the resin is thickly laid, then it is necessary to stir in the mixture by using the brush on the mould like a pallette knife on a pallette. Brush out smoothly after mixing.

Clean the brush.

LITERATURE

So far this chapter has been a series of notes concerning the background to building a G.R.P. canoe. There are some direct instructions which will be helpful with the KW 7, and other similar sized boats. In order to read about how to build the boat, stage by stage, you are advised to read the following :

How to Build a Glass Fibre Canoe, Trylon Ltd, Thrift Street, Wollaston, Northamptonshire, NN9 7QJ.

Canoe Building in GRP Alan Byde, A. & C. Black Ltd, 4 Soho Square, London W1.

Canoe Design and Construction Alan Byde, Pelham Books, 52 Bedford Square, London WC1B 3EF.

And, I have no doubt at all, most of the suppliers offering materials to canoe builders have their own advice to offer.

THE MANUFACTURERS

Finally, a little bit of history to round off. Around 1962-5 a few people were beginning to build G.R.P. canoes in schools and youth clubs, but with no help in the way of moulds being available, or advice in print. I was one of them. A few people were 'pirating' commercial moulds, that is taking moulds off without permission. The manufacturers were very annoyed, and now I've made a few, I can sympathise. The work necessary to make a boat from the idea is a long tedious business. Around 1968-70 a few manufacturers made moulds available to the few selected clubs. But the amateurs had learned how to build moulds, and so they could supply moulds of a sort, but not very good in terms of high polish, or smooth unrippled finish. One firm, Trylon, advertised under a dramatic cartoon of a pirate, cutlass in teeth, patch over eye, that they welcomed pirates. I helped Trylon to make moulds available, and their first one was the Tiger, which has proved very useful. This was followed by the BAT Mk 2 and the OX 1. I am told that possibly a thousand OX 1s were built in 1970.

However, all this pressure from the amateurs to get better boats has persuaded the manufacturers to make out-of-date moulds available, and this is raising the standard of canoe construction in Britain very considerably. As more and more youngsters go afloat because more and more 'class' boats are available, then more and more become very good and go to the manufacturers for better boats. Style plays a considerable part in top-class competition, too, so obsolescence is frequent.

Few top-class canoes ever become obsolescent, because the demands of top-class competition wrecks boats as fast as they can be supplied.

CHAPTER NINE

Basic Canoeing Strokes, and Exercises

This section could be written in many ways, but it seems to me that the better way is to write it as if I were in fact taking you on a novice course from the Centre of which I am warden. It is, therefore, written as advice to a person in charge of a group, and as direct instruction to the members of the group, but despite the accent on the group and on a particular place, the advice is suitable for the individual, too.

So this chapter is offered to the beginner. Be critical, but try the work suggested. There are hidden intentions in the work. The emphasis on rafting up, for example, bores one of my critics. Yet I know that if a person is given the job, repeatedly, of trying to line up with some other moving object, then the effort of the intellect which is required, is very instructive. The intention is not to produce people who are good at rafting up, but to develop a frame of mind that starts off by perceiving an aim, and then in achieving it. Give simple problems, offer a chance of success, and the effort of learning to canoe becomes fun.

If it is fun, it is worth doing, and if it is worth doing, it should be done safely. With safety assured, then the discipline of trying and trying yet again is required. With such discipline, the challenges can be faced.

Several basic concepts about handling a canoe have become established in my mind. The first I came to was embodied in the four words: fun, safety, discipline, challenge.

The next is illustrated by the canoe in the sphere. Imagine

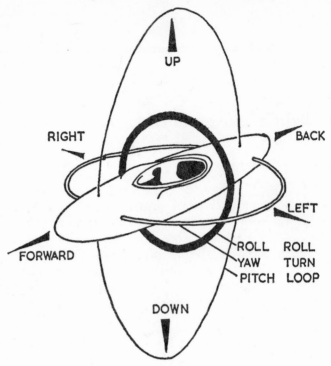

THREE DIMENSION : DIRECTION & ROTATION.

a sphere with three axes of rotation, and three directions of movement along these axes. These are as follows:

STRAIGHT LINE MOVEMENTS
1. Straight forward and backward – Initiated by canoeist.
2. Directly sideways, right and left – Initiated by canoeist.
3. Straight up and down – Initiated by water.

TURNING MOVEMENTS
1. Rotation horizontally, i.e. turning – Initiated by canoeist.
2. Rotation laterally, i.e. rolling – Initiated by canoeist.
3. Rotation end over end, i.e. looping – Initiated by water.
   The sequence of teaching I find develops as follows.
Straight line, 1. Rotation, 1; Straight line, 2. Rotation, 2.
And one learns to deal with stage three in each case.

74

Basic Canoeing Strokes, and Exercises

The difference between basic strokes and movements and advanced strokes and movements is summarised as follows:

A basic stroke is one which manoeuevres the canoe, accurately and simply, with the canoeist's weight taken by the upright canoe.

An advanced stroke is one in which the canoe is manoeuevered with power, subtlety, and with the paddler's weight taken by the paddle blade.

Two or three basic identifiable strokes can be assimilated into one advanced move of great power and grace so that they seem like one stroke; it is from the basic work that mastery develops and satisfaction in something well done is experienced.

I offer the following progression of skills to my novice groups.

First Session, $1\frac{1}{2}$ to 2 hours.

1. Carrying canoe to water. Check equipment, especially life-jackets.
2. Entering canoe.
3. Sitting properly in it.
4. Rafting up.
5. Basic forward paddling, including emergency stops.
6. Short journey, about 400 yds. Identify weak paddlers.
7. Turning strokes.
8. Capsize drill, including rescue method, swim across river and back.
9. How to empty a canoe.
10. Return equipment to shed.

Second Session, $1\frac{1}{2}$ to 2 hours.

1. Reiterate last session's work, brief practice, no capsizes.
2. Draw stroke.
3. Support stroke.
4. One-mile trip to low weir (3 ft. high).
5. Correction of paddling strokes, selecting tail-end paddler and coaching him forward, then taking the next, and so on.
6. Shoot weir, using support stroke.
7. Portage, relaunch by seal slide on grass bank.

8. Return. Capsize, rescues, swim.
9. Replace equipment on racks.

Third Session, 2 hours.
1. Reiterate last session's work, brief practice, no capsizes.
2. Short journey, talking about points of interest, about 2–3 miles.
3. Coach and correct faults in progress.
4. Return, play about, swapping places in canoes in deep water, rescue drills, capsizes, swimming.
5. Return equipment to racks.

These novice instruction sessions usually take place during warmer weather, when the water in the Thames is tolerable for young swimmers. That is, between May and October. From October to May we are usually working indoors in a swimming bath.

The follow-up to this work is to persuade young and able canoeists to take out small groups of people who have been on the novice course, and take them on short evening trips. In Oxford we have dozens of these alternative journeys, short or long, easy or difficult, smooth or rough according to taste. After a period of improving on basic work, we set out to teach more advanced work. This tends not to be so clearly patterned as the basic work, and goes a little as follows.

Improver's Work*
1. Rescue methods, both as rescuer and rescued.
2. Low telemark.
3. High telemark.
4. Sculling actions.
5. Playing about with weir spouts and stoppers.
6. Break in and break out (cut in, cut out) on fast-moving water.
7. Ferry glide.
8. 'Waltzing' on spout.
9. Stopper traps, and ways of making escape.
10. Rolling.

*Not detailed in this book. For this, see *Living Canoeing*.

11. Canoe polo, wiggle test, simple competitions.
12. Weekend canoe camp on river or sea.

The full progression through this work will take a whole summer season for the average beginner, but by the end of that time they are usually very able in canoes and quite competent to judge water movements and whether weirs are safe or not, and whether they can take on some journey or not. By the next season, especially if they have by then built their own glass reinforced plastic boat, they are usually fully equipped and ready to make extensive journeys, or take part in high-quality competition, quite on their own and without supervision.

The description of work that follows is related to kayaks on a river of the nature of the Thames. Other places and other people require emphasis on entirely other things. It is not possible to relate all that can be done in this short chapter; however, what follows is what we do with fair success for many scores of users of the Centre each year.

CARRYING THE CANOE

One may carry the average semi-lightweight canoe quite easily on the shoulder. Adults have no trouble. Children under the age of fifteen, more or less, find this weight awkward to carry as their shoulders have not yet developed sufficiently to square up under a weight of thirty to thirty-five pounds. The method is as follows :

1. Place the canoe on the ground and point it in the direction you want it to go, cockpit uppermost.
2. Kneel beside it on the left side, knees beside the cockpit.
3. Reach across with the right hand, palm upwards, curl fingers under far side cockpit rim just in front of the seat hip flange.
4. Reach across body with left hand, grasp left side of cockpit rim and hitch the canoe sideways up on to the slope of the right thigh.
Note : The two following movements should be synchronised.
5. Duck the right shoulder down, crook the right arm and get the canoe up on to the point of the shoulder so that the right side cockpit rim rests on the right shoulder, as close to

the thick neck muscle as possible. Use the upthrust of the right hand to ease the weight of the canoe on the shoulder.

6. Stand up, using the thrust of the thigh muscles.

7. Later, there is no need to kneel, simply stoop over, and with what seems to be an effortless flick, the whole canoe is flipped up on to the shoulder. It's a knack.

8. The paddle should be lying on the ground alongside the canoe. Hook the left toe under the centre of the shaft. With an upward flick of the toe lift the paddle up into the left hand. This takes practice, but becomes easy after a while.

CHECKING THE LIFEJACKET

Assuming that this is the BSS 3595 type, then I check the following items before anyone in my charge goes afloat. Remember that wearing a lifejacket, in my opinion, is not a certain safeguard. Some knowledge of why and when is also required.

1. Waist tape properly fastened, harness firm but not too tight.

2. Inflation tube has cap properly fixed.

3. Lifejacket deflated in normal use.

4. Lifting becket, if fitted, fixed on its stud.

5. Neck strap pulling back of neck piece down out of the way.

CHECKING THE SPRAY DECK

1. The spray deck must fit the canoe being used.

2. There must be some method of releasing it, a tape, cord, or loop.

3. The stitching must be sound, the elasticated rim firm.

4. Ensure that the centre rear seam is dead centre, or fitting it to the cockpit rim becomes very difficult.

CHECKING THE PADDLE

1. Sound condition; correct length (see diagram).

CHECKING THE BOAT

1. Suitable for beginners.

78

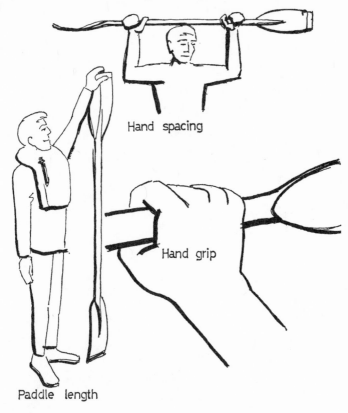

Hand spacing

Hand grip

Paddle length

2. Good condition; no serious leaks; comfortable seat.
3. Buoyancy blocks fitted.
4. No footrest fixed (this comes later).
5. End loop or toggles fitted.
6. Thames Conservancy Licence in place.

ENTERING THE CANOE

There are two basic ways of going afloat:

1(a). Launch canoe. (b) Get into it.
2(a). Get into canoe. (b) Launch both.

The first method is described here. Getting out is the same, but taken in reverse order.

1. Stand with canoe on shoulder at side of water.

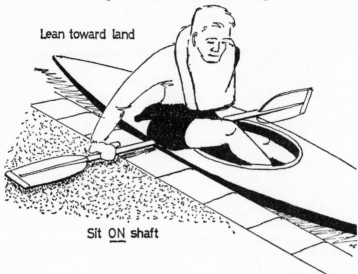

Lean toward land

Sit <u>ON</u> shaft

2. Stretch out the right leg at an angle, take weight on left leg.

3. Right toes should be pointing to water, toes over edge of landing.

4. Slide canoe off shoulder, let stern slip into water, hull slides down thigh.

5. Release grasp on cockpit rim, get hold of end loop, lower into water. Bows should be pointing upstream.

6. Use paddle as a boat hook. Do *not* launch paddle with canoe. Steady canoe in water by placing paddle tip on canoe bottom inside cockpit.

7. Place paddle across both canoe deck at rear of cockpit, and landing edge. Landside blade should be flat, waterside blade up and down.

8. Crouch down beside cockpit, paddle shaft behind. Sit *on* shaft.

9. Put waterside hand on shaft, thumb over shaft, fingers grasping cockpit rim, curled inside centre rear of cockpit rim. Thumb is toward the body.

10. Landside hand palm down across paddle shaft.

11. Transfer feet into canoe. Lean back, take weight on hands.

12. Leaning backwards, slide arched body down into cockpit.

13. Sit up straight, hitch behind into comfortable place in seat.

14. Now bring paddle around the body in front, ready for use.

N.B. There are other ways, but this is good for beginners.

SITTING IN THE CANOE

1. Sit up straight. Lean very slightly forward. *Note:* One usually leans in the direction in which one intends to go when canoeing.

2. Fit spray deck, ensure release strap or cord is outside the deck ready for use. Fit it, centre rear, then sides at the rear, centre front, then sides at the front. It goes on better from the back toward the front than the other way.

3. Look for the 'jelly-bottoms.' This happens to one in five first time out. There is a great deal of tension, and the person over-corrects. This sets up an oscillation in the canoe, a trembling really. This shows in the water around as a series of tiny ripples spreading outwards from the hull. Point this out to the paddler, and the mere fact of realisation is enough to stop this tremble in almost everyone.

4. Rest paddle across front of cockpit. Check :

a. grasp correct.

b. paddle central in hands.

c. if right handed feathering, right blade up and down, left blade horizontal.

5. Look all around. Check where the other traffic on the river is and in which direction it is heading.

RAFTING UP

The group, in my case often not less than six, is persuaded to gather around into a 'Raft'. No instruction is given in how to paddle or manoeuvre the boat. One simply has a task to perform, and tries to do it. No coaching is given unless someone is clearly in real trouble. The idea is to give the group a focus, and let them each work out their own way of making it.

1. Nominate a person raft centre.

2. One paddler comes alongside, generally from behind, and lays beside the raft centre, facing the same way.

3. The others all come alongside one at a time until each person is grasping the cockpit rim of the canoe alongside.

4. The end person has his paddle in both hands, and he is held into the raft by the single-handed grasp of the person next to the end.

5. The right-hand man and the left-hand man are nominated.

6. The raft is manoeuvred on the instructions of someone. could be the person on the bank, or the raft centre. Instructions as follow :

a. Going ahead. 'Left and right, paddle forwards'

b. Going astern. 'Left and right, paddle backwards.'

c. Turning to right. 'Left forward, right reverse.'

d. Turning to left. 'Right forward, left reverse.'

7. Select a place on the bank and go to it.

8. Break up the raft and reform with new centre and ends. Do it again.

FORWARD AND BACKWARD PADDLING

After the rafting session, about fifteen minutes, people are beginning to grasp the essential ways of controlling a raft, and so a canoe. They then split up and paddle around generally, but out of the way of other river craft. Given river space, I do the following.

1. All members of the group, backs to the bank, stern touching the bank (which ensures that they are all in a neat straight line, looking outwards at the river, tucked close in to the bank and thus out of the way). This is a basic starting position for almost everything that follows.

2. Brief demo, paddling forwards and stopping and paddling backwards and stopping. As follows.

3a. Sit up straight.

b. Lean forward slightly.

c. Reach forward with right paddle blade.

d. Right arm straight.

e. Left arm bent, hand at shoulder level.

f. Right shoulder forward.

g. Blade into water beside hull.

h. Straighten left arm, pull back with straight right arm.

i. Turn shoulders so left shoulder leads, right shoulder back.

j. Right hand alongside hip, lift blade out of water, arm bends.

k. Left arm straight, left shoulder leading, action repeats with left changed for right, as above.

STOPPING

When some speed has been gained, obviously quite slow at first, then practise emergency stopping. You have hydraulic disc brakes. The discs are at the end of the paddle shaft, the hydraulics are all around you.

1. Command 'Stop'.

2. Drop right blade into water, blade up and down, hold firm against water pressure momentarily.

3. Chop blade out of water, drop left blade in similarly, hold and brace momentarily. Chop out.

4. Right blade behind body and sweep down deep into water and forward against water pressure.

PADDLE "HIGH"

EFFICIENT PADDLING

BLADE CLOSE TO HULL

LEAN FORWARD

OPEN FINGERS

CLIP OUT BY HIP

5. Chop out, left blade deep into water and push forward against water pressure.

Avoid these faults:

a. Blade not at right angles to movement. Cuts away under canoe and over you go.

b. First two strikes hit water, blade twists in hand and skips over surface, no effective braking.

c. Holding first two strikes too long. Canoe swerves all over the place, straight line stopping impossible.

d. Failing to stop movement completely *related to the bank*. Stopping relative to the current is easy, but people fail to notice how the bank is slipping away past them until it is pointed out.

GOING BACKWARDS

Remember, one leans in the direction in which one is going, and a good lookout is necessary. I look for the following points.

1. Look over the shoulder to see what is behind.

2. Stop. Look again. Lean backwards.

3. Reach right paddle back towards the stern, drive paddle deep down and forward past the right side. Hand level with knees, lift blade out.

4. As above on left side. Keep going. Keep looking.

STOPPING IN REVERSE

This is easy; simply paddle forwards. However, this churns up great gouts of water which fly back over the boat and into the face. Stopping when going forward slings water out in front, which is a handy dodge if one is playing the fool and wants to wet a passing punter, but watch out, some have long poles. But stopping in reverse is a self-drenching exercise.

A SHORT JOURNEY

Trying to teach people to keep a canoe in a straight line is like telling someone in a classroom how to ride a bicycle. There is only one way, try it. I find the better way now is to spot a place to go to, say two hundred yards away in clear view, then I set off at full speed shouting 'follow me!' This has its dangers because my back is to the group, but I make sure there are no other river craft bearing down on us before I set off. Given an average group of six or ten, I find one or two right on my stern, working well, looking eager. A little way back is another trying hard. Behind that are two more looking a little lost and swerving about. Right at the start, or even further away than that, is some desperate soul engaged in ramming the bank repeatedly. Directional stability has eluded him.

The two who are close behind me, I ask to remain there and wait for the others and help them if they can. This forms a gathering point. I return full speed to the wandering one, and instruct as follows.

1. Stop. Just drift.
2. Explain the correction aspect of each stroke as well as its driving power.
3. Go through forward paddling instruction.
4. Explain as follows: 'If you swerve to the left, paddle forward on the left. If to the right, paddle forward on the right. Bring the paddle right around to the back end each time until the swerve ceases. Paddle only on that side until the swerve ceases.'
5. 'Off you go'. Set out for the group. I try to keep instruction to a minimum, as confusion very soon overtakes a person in this difficulty. I may put in a few words as follows. 'Right! Correct right. And again. Right around to the back, O.K. No more. Catch it, its sliding left now. Left and left again. You will improve as you learn to correct sooner and not to overcorrect. Its like driving a sliding motor-car on ice.'
6. As we go along getting nearer to the group, we may overtake another laggard. I leave the first one to his or her own chances, and then concentrate on the next one.
7. By the time the group has gathered at the rally point, most will be saying, 'how the heck does one keep this skittish little beast in a straight line?' When my group asks me a direct question from experience, they really want to know, and now I can teach them.
8. The group is then made to put their back ends on the

river bank, stuck on the mud, or backed up to the Sea Scouts' jetty, so that they are all in a line looking out toward the river. This manoeuvring takes a long long time at first, but it's worth it. A great deal of basic learning is going on with all these small tasks to do. In future my request will be 'Backs to the bank', and in this way the atmosphere for a teaching interlude is established. I try not to 'teach' for more than five minutes in ten.

TURNING STROKES

With the group lined up watching, I show them the sweep turn. The instructions refer to placing the paddle, not to the resulting movement of the canoe.

1. There are four sweep turns, right or left, forwards or backwards.

2. The right forward sweep goes like this.

3. Right paddle blade in the water alongside the right bow. Blade vertical, driving face of blade facing outwards. Right arm stretched out straight, right shoulder well forward, left arm bent left hand about level with left shoulder point.

4. Place blade half in water, swing as wide out from canoe as it can go, keeping right arm straight. Try to touch back of canoe with blade. Left hand moves across to right side of cockpit front.

5. To do this, keep your eyes on the right blade, swing your shoulders so that the left shoulder is forward and the right shoulder to the rear. A lot of body twist should be used. Try and get shoulder points in line with the canoe *Keep your right arm straight.*

6. Repeat gently and thoughtfully, turn completely around an imaginary pivot slightly away to your left. The canoe moves on the circumference of a circle. The more manoeuvrable the canoe, the smaller the circle. The less manoeuvrable, the wider the circle.

7. Try a forward left sweep turn. Same as before, only on the other side. *Keep the left arm straight.*

8. Now a reverse right sweep turn. Same as for forward sweep, only start at the end and finish at the beginning. *Keep the right arm straight.*

9. Left reverse sweep turn.

10. All practise each of these four moves for five to ten minutes.

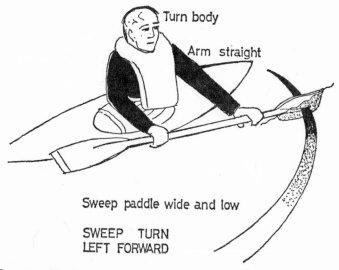

Turn body

Arm straight

Sweep paddle wide and low

SWEEP TURN
LEFT FORWARD

TURNING VARIATIONS

With the group back to the bank again, watching, the following moves are shown to them.

Forward and Reverse Sweep Turn

The paddle is used alternately forward on one side and backward on the other side. In this turn the canoe pivots over a point under the cockpit, and it matters not whether the canoe is manoeuvrable or not, it will turn in that one place. The more readily the canoe turns the less time it takes to turn around. This move is quite often used by all manner of canoeists.

Correction Sweep

When the canoe begins to swerve, the bows will start to swing to, say, the left. If one is listening, a slight increase in the bubbling noise at the stern will be noticed. This shows that the stern is swinging, skidding really, to the right. It is possible to notice the stern break away before noticing the bow swing. This is common with the majority of canoes which tend to be stern turning, i.e. the stern turns more readily than the bows. However, some recent slalom kayaks are bow turning, and so their characteristic turn is quite different. However, the beginner will curse either with equal fluency and lack of understanding.

The correction stroke is demonstrated as follows.

1. Paddle forward. I paddle toward you from across the river. You see my bows are swinging to the left.

2. I do not break paddling rhythm, but instead of keeping the left blade close to the boat, it is carried wide away from the hull and what was a driving stroke is converted into the second half of a left forward sweep turn, blade vertical. Keep the paddling rhythm going. Swerve stops, but beware of overcorrection.

Capsize drill

This depends on the weather. If the water is frigidly cold, I might postpone capsize instruction until later in the year. The risks of a deliberate capsize in shockingly cold water must be set against the risks of a capsize by a novice with no previous experience when alone; but sometimes a decision must be made. I can make this decision knowing that hot showers await the returning soaked canoeist. In summer the river can be like a warm bath and it is often a pleasure to flop in and swim about anyway. The drill goes as follows.

1. This drill which you will practise may be of little use in a

ROLL FORWARD TO GET OUT

capsize. In a real emergency you may make a real hash of it and you could be in some haste, panic even. But practise carefully, and your mind will become calmed in the future difficulty. Listen and watch, don't do anything.

2. Paddle in both hands, normal grasp. Bring paddle shaft to (say) right side of boat, shaft horizontal and parallel to right side. Lean forward and aim forehead at knuckles of left hand.

3. Still holding paddle, lunge forward, going off balance over the paddle shaft to the right. Wait one moment underwater. Let go of paddle, with left hand. Pull off spray deck with left hand. Roll out forward, curled up forward. Got it? Forward! ! ! People coming out leaning backwards tend to break in the middle, and leave skin behind on the cockpit rim, so curl up forward. Please!

4. Emerging beside the canoe, get hold of three things, yourself, the canoe and the paddle – in that order. Go to the end of the canoe. *Leave it upside down*: Do not attempt to right it. Do not rest on it.

5. Right. Now you've seen it done, one at a time, practise.

CAPSIZE PRACTICE

The group pairs off. I like to see one person at a time capsizing, with his partner watching him, and if the partner thinks he has been under too long or seems in any way to be in trouble, he will tell me. But if no more than one in the group is going over at one time then I shall be watching anyway.

The first paddler goes over and I watch with great care. I wait until the person is once again re-oriented, and then I give helpful criticism. With this first capsize in the series, I stop at this point and explain the first rescue ('X' system, q. v.). I show how important it is to avoid loading the boat with water. I put the paddler back in the boat. All the time I'm looking out for other river craft. The average 'X' rescue takes me about two to four minutes, depending on how much water is in the boat, how much talking I do, and how much the Fingal (q. v.) factor is in evidence.

The capsizes then follow in order, one after the other, the

people then go to the bank using a leg-kick backstroke and pulling the canoe upside down behind them, and with help they tip it out on the bank. They then take off the spray deck, and after all the capsizes have finished they re-enter the water and swim across the river and back. I always have one person, either myself or another paddler, to escort them across and back. They wear the lifejacket, and it is remarkable how difficult it is to swim in a lifejacket.

As soon as the swim is over, they carry their canoes back to the store, and go and shower and change into dry clothes.

RETURNING EQUIPMENT TO THE SHED

The condition of the canoes and equipment must be good. If anything were to go wrong, there would be a professional responsibility on me in addition to the usual canoeing skill and responsibility. I might have to face the coroner, a bereaved parent, my employers, and worst of all myself . . . so sometimes I 'blow my top' when some unthinking youngster fails to put the gear away properly. Think why, if you will.

1. Empty the canoe. Put it on the rack where it belongs.
2. Rack the paddles.
3. Hang up the lifejackets. In numerical order please.
4. Hang up the spray decks to dry, or the stitches rot.
5. Sweep out the shed. (Faint hope!)
6. Collect all your wet clothing and take it home. Wash clothing in clean water. River water is corrosive, and it smells after two hot days in a car boot, like some dreadful horror unburied. Sea water is also alive with little living organisms, and when they die in stale sea water, even though the clothing has dried, as soon as it gets wet again, why, even your best friends will tell you. Stay down wind of them for mercy's sake.

Final point. Some canoes are found to be leaking in use, and one gets a youngster with a wet bottom and a real source of complaint. This canoe must be put in the workshop on the 'For repair' rack, with a felt pen mark where the trouble is. In a busy summer it simply gets a sticky tape patch at short notice, but a real workshop job means several days drying out.

Basic Canoeing Strokes, and Exercises

SECOND SESSION, 1½ to 2 hours

The first thing to do is to tell the group what it will be doing. The next thing is to let them go afloat and to practise the following things. No instruction is required.

1. Carrying canoe to water, and launching it.
2. Entering canoe, adjusting spray deck.
3. Forming raft. Manoeuvring raft.
4. Breaking up, reforming.
5. Paddle over short journey again.
6. Continue with new session.

DRAW STROKE

In this the canoe is made to go sideways. By careful use of the paddle the canoe can be made to go diagonally and to go sideways with an element of turning in it. Not only can the canoe be pulled toward the blade in the water, it can

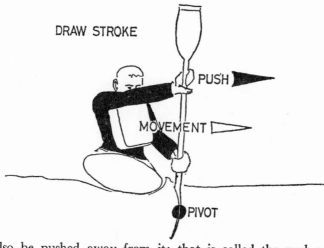

DRAW STROKE

PUSH

MOVEMENT

PIVOT

also be pushed away from it; that is called the push-over, or in the States, the pry-away. In any case it is a little advanced, and a good do-it-yourself capsize exercise.

1. Take paddle in normal grasp.
2. Place, (say) right blade flat on water, shaft at right angles to centre of canoe, right arm straight, shaft held low across front of body.
3. Slowly and gently, press the blade down into the water,

and raise the left hand to shoulder height on the left side.

4. Now start to rotate the body toward the right, left shoulder turning across, right shoulder down toward the rear. Left elbow high.

5. Push with the left hand in the direction in which you want to travel.

6. Almost immediately you will find that the blade is going under the boat and you are in danger of tripping over it. Turn the blade at right angles, to take any sideways pressure off it. Slice the blade back toward where it came from, out to the right about three feet.

7. Return to the state in (1) above. Repeat.

In the first few tentative pulls the paddle will be almost out of the water, but as confidence grows, take the blade much deeper, so that the right hand is under water. One does not alter the position of the hands on the shaft at all throughout this exercise. Try this on the left side now, and then even, if you feel able, a pry-away, or a diagonal move; more likely one will be seeking ways of correcting an accidental diagonal movement.

The faults are usually as follow :

1. Trips over blade. Get the release right with paddle tight alongside boat by cockpit. If a trip seems inevitable, let go the shaft. This is a rather useless thing to do as one should be hanging on to the paddle come what may; but in the first few nervous minutes it is permissible, under protest, to drop the paddle.

2. Withdrawing with top hand. The top hand, instead of

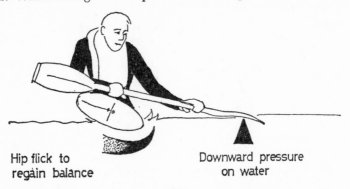

Hip flick to
regain balance

Downward pressure
on water

firmly pushing in the required direction, is withdrawn away from the required direction.

3. Reversed hand grip. Many beginners take the top hand off the paddle and reverse the grasp, so that the thumb is toward the blade instead of the body. Correct this at once.

4. The line of the draw is not in line with the centre of lateral pressure of the boat. The result is that the action presents a reduced sideways movement with a turning component. If the stern leads, the action is directed too much toward the rear. If the bow leads, then the action is being carried too far forward. The corrections are then obvious.

SUPPORT STROKE

After practising the above for about five to ten minutes the group puts its backs to the bank and the next action is explained.

1. Place the right paddle blade (say) out as for the draw stroke. Drive face downwards.

2. Lift the blade about one foot off the water.

3. Tuck the knees in firmly under the side decks. Sit up.

4. Lean very slightly toward the blade above the water. Slap the blade gently on to the water. Sit upright again.

5. Put blade down on to water. Sink it deeply, so that it is about two to three feet deep. Rotate the shaft through 90° so that the blade can be slipped edgeways up through the water back above the surface where it is wanted. Practise this several times as quickly as possible, trying to pluck the blade out of the water in a swift chopping move upwards.

6. Go back to four above. Lean further over, use a definite downthrust on the shaft with the right hand to regain the upright balance.

7. Keep practising. Try and get the right elbow wet, then the right shoulder, or, if the canoeist is very good and the water is warm, even duck the head under and rise up. This is almost a roll.

SHORT JOURNEY, TWO

From the teaching place, I take the group about 400 yards to the two bridges, where they wait until I get there and I am satisfied that they are safe to cross this very busy part of the Thames. We go down under the upstream arch and wait on the left bank just above the weir spill on the right bank. I must mention that Thames Conservancy regulations prohibit any vessel going over the weir, but this is where the local children play in the water, the swing on ropes and slide down the mossy slope of the weir face in summer whooping and yelling; as I have said, there are some weirs which are fun and some which are killers. You need to know which is which.

Up to the two bridges I follow the group, keeping the stragglers as far forward as I can, always concentrating on the rearmost person. From the two bridges down to the weir I am in front, ready to stop anyone going over prematurely. I make the following points:

1. Keep out from under bushes. Underwater is a network of roots and trapped rubbish. A waterflow as slight as half-a-mile per hour can hold the submerged body against this entanglement until it drowns. Never hold on to overhanging branches.

2. In floods this water runs about 3 to 4 m.p.h. That is between four and six feet per second. The nearest radial weir, the dangerous treble radial, is about two hundred yards away, that's six hundred feet, or one hundred seconds at fastest flow. You would have less than two minutes to get out of this stream at that flow before going over the edge. It's nasty, so be careful!

3. See that weir? It is concrete and there is a thin skin of water flowing down it. That weir is in the shape of a wave on a surfing beach about to break. When you are surfing, your boat is planing; it no longer goes through the water, it goes over it. That is what you will do when you go over this weir. So what we have is a surfing wave in concrete. This is where you start to learn to surf.

4. To shoot the weir, go downstream about twenty feet. Paddle upstream, angling in toward the weir at about 30 degrees from the line of the top of the weir. Paddle hard, as you must shove the boat over the shallow water at the top of the weir. As you go over trail the paddle behind, as in the

94

support stroke, blade flat, lying toward the topside of the weir. Wallop! Down you go. I will wait for you, come one at a time when you are ready.

And over they come. We portage on the high bank side where the diving hole is, and for the first time the group tries the seal launch, endways on, into the diving hole off the slippery wet grass. They then may try again and again to shoot the weir. There are six basic ways: straight forwards, straight backwards; (but neither on this weir); sideways, right, bow leading; sideways, left, bow leading; and sideways left, stern leading; and sideways right, stern leading.

SEAL LAUNCH

1. Line up the canoe endways on (but only on a slippery surface like wet grass or mud, or even clean, wet, rounded pebbles).
2. Climb in, taking care not to slide off before you are ready.
3. Adjust spray deck, paddle tucked under right arm-pit and in right hand. Left-hand knuckles down on to grass.
4. Push off smartly into the water, using left-hand knuckles and right paddle blade like a crutch to ease the canoe over the drop. Lean well forward and urge the canoe downwards and forwards into the water. The water swills right up the foredeck to the cockpit then the bows rise and away you go. Too slow, and you will hang up with the stern caught on the bank and the bows in the water, and you capsize in mid-air, rather difficult, but excruciatingly funny for the watchers.

After we have had enough time here we return to the Centre. The group is reminded of the rescue work we have done, (there have probably been a few accidental capsizes already), and a rescue session begins right by the Centre. Everyone must perform both as rescuer and rescued, and this is a wet and hilarious time usually. Another across river swim, and return the kit to the store. Then a hot shower, and dry clothes.

THIRD SESSION

All begins as before. We go through the technical strokes quite quickly. Then a favourite journey is up to Folly Bridge, exploring the arches and backwaters, and return. Alternatively, we go around the 3½ miles of the backwaters, shooting the Lasher Weir on the way, and taking in Iffley Weir spout on the way back, with attendant capsizes and rescues in deep water. Portage over the rollers, and back to the Centre. By this time more than half the group is 'hooked' on canoeing. They then start to learn to be canoeists. That is good, but just as good is the knowledge that those who do not become enthusiastic canoeists straight away have at least had an introduction to it, and know where to begin.

You have read what I have to say about the surf ski. As a starting craft for anyone it is hard to beat. Shorter versions of the ski exist. There is the solo rescue ski, about 10 feet long, and the double short ski, about 12 feet long. Both these have a serious purpose, in assisting beach lifeguards to avoid loss of life. They are also first-class fun boats, and the beginner simply climbs on and sets off. Carrying the ski is simply a matter of clutching the tree in the crook of the arm, and carrying it on the hip; the spray deck is not required; p.80 goes into some detail on how to get into a kayak cockpit, which is not now required. Capsize drill is as easy as falling off a log. That's all you need to know. The various strokes are the same. To launching I would add, launching the ski, then swimming to it and scrambling on, like climbing over a wall. There is a knack in sitting on the ski cockpit, then swinging the leg over the tree to sit properly upon it. In short, the introduction to kayaking is much easier via the surf ski, with fewer problems for the person in charge, and one built-in trap is absent entirely. The legs are not within a cockpit.

CHAPTER TEN

Baths Canoeing

What is a swimming bath? A place for swimmers only, or possibly a place for canoeing practice as well? Many baths supervisors recognise that this extension of the use of a baths is legitimate.

Some people may attempt to carry the argument a little further, and say that sailing dinghies could also appear in swimming baths; well they do, and I have seen them there, but for strictly defined purposes. There is a proper limit to what is reasonable in an indoor swimming bath, length 25 metres, width 10 metres, but special forms of canoeing are possible, and legitimate, and enjoyable.

The use of swimming baths as canoeing pools is fairly recent. Many school pools were built in the sixties, so development before then was rare. Initially the pools were used as places where demonstrations of canoeing skill were given as an interlude in swimming galas. Then they were used as places where fairly skilled canoeists learned to roll kayaks as the Eskimos did. In 1959 I was one of about six people in the north-east of England who could roll a kayak. Now you could find more than that number in one school, or even in one age-group in a school.

Developing from that, as these activities were accepted, it became reasonable to use valuable time to help beginners to begin in some comfort and peace and safety. Now this is the major part of our work at the Centre in the school baths which we use.

Because many beginners began using swimming baths, the

pressures on time and space became important. It didn't take long for several people to recognise the need for a special small canoe for baths use for training beginners, and for teaching rolling skills. This is basically a slalom type cockpit in the smallest craft that will support a full-grown adult on the water. These first baths canoes were often sawn-off, Eskimo-type kayaks.

Pressure on the space available led to smaller canoes, but these were found to be much more sensitive to small changes of design, and so improved designs were brought out. It was very much a trial-and-error situation, at least so far as I was concerned, but repeated efforts brought forth canoes which are suitable for teaching beginners to begin, improvers to roll, and games players to play a most skilful, colourful, and exciting sport, canoe polo. Stunt canoeing flourishes, too, with wild characters hurtling off high diving boards, from three metres at most, into 14 feet of water at least. This is now a respectable activity as John Noakes of B.B.C. Television's 'Blue Peter' has done it at Crystal Palace baths. If anyone has first tried this indoors, then the later frightening drop over the face of a curling ten-foot surf breaker is not quite so paralysing in its effect on the mind.

Well, that is a brief history of the development of baths canoeing so far. The point is that baths canoeing, not only as a preparation for outdoor canoeing but also as an end in itself, is well worth developing; it will continue to develop, too.

Three-Session Baths Course, Novices

First we need the correct equipment. This should be six baths canoes, six spray decks with release straps, six short paddles and for the first session, several lifejackets and a plastic football. The bath canoes are about seven to eight feet long, twenty-two inches wide, and have round ends. They are made of glass reinforced plastic, and when hung on their hooks on the wall at the side they positively enhanced the appearance of the baths with their bright colours.

Baths Canoeing

Briefly, the course members don't want to listen to a lot of talk, so let them get on with it, and they *will* learn when they come to you *asking* for help.

Begin by checking whether they can swim. In canoeing when an accident has occurred, and deep-water rescue is needed, then it is an advantage if the canoeist has become used to the banging about that rough water will give to canoes, and the people in the water beside them. Canoes are remarkably hard objects, and one can collect a thick ear in the water alongside when a canoe swings violently across.

The canoes are lined up along the bath at right angles to the line of swim. The course members will all swim six lengths, straight away, and will either swim under, or over each canoe, alternately as they come to it. If there are assistants around to hold the canoes steady, so much the better. It is useful for the assistants without paddles, to sit in the canoes to keep them on station, as the balancing exercises needed as hefty course members hurl themselves over the fore or rear deck are very good at developing lightning reflexes. My assistants are usually last year's beginners.

A brief demonstration follows, showing a capsize and swimmer-to-canoeist rescue, and a capsize and exit. Half the course members now get into the canoes, and the other half watch.

Without spray deck or paddle they then paddle around the bath, using their hands only. Some people can whizz a boat about inside five minutes using very sophisticated hand-paddling strokes: but put a paddle there and it's months before that fluency begins to show again. On request they all go to the deep end and, *one at a time,* they capsize under the careful eye of the coach. It is important that only one actually capsizes at a time, and this is true for open waters especially.

Then the boats are emptied out. At one time I made this a big point and took time over it, but usually the group will pick up the various methods of emptying out a canoe if they are shown this in the course of work.

99

The people change over and the second half group does the same work. About fifteen minutes have passed, and now the spray decks are put on, and the lifejackets are introduced (Although we don't usually use lifejackets in a swimming pool because the chlorine rots the materials, making them unsafe for use outside, and in the baths many of the situations which require lifejackets are, in any case, avoided).

The fully equipped canoeists get into the canoes and, with paddle in hand for the first time, take their first tentative prods with the blade to move themselves about. Let them get on with it, don't lecture interminably about how to hold the shaft and so on. After a few minutes stop them, and command as follows :

1. Put down your paddle.
2. Release your spray deck.
3. Check your lifejacket, straps firm, air valve cap on.
4. Capsize (*one at a time*).
5. Swim to shallow end using a back stroke, towing the canoe by its end toggle.
6. Re-enter, and, with spray deck properly on and paddle in hand.
7. Capsize again, releasing spray deck under water (*one at a time*).
8. Hand over for the other half group.

By this time there is only about fifteen minutes left out of an hour session. The lifejackets are now put aside, and later washed with clean water which does not have chlorine in it, and they are then returned to the Centre as they will not be used again for this course in the baths.

There follows a brief demonstration on how to paddle forward and how to stop, and how to paddle backwards. Each half group has about five minutes in which to practise this simple manoeuvre. The boats and equipment are now put away, and that is roughly forty-five minutes gone in a one-hour session. The other fifteen minutes is of course, as all baths organisers well know, necessary for getting the people into and out of the changing rooms before the next group arrives.

SESSION TWO

This starts as before with an-under-and-over session, and the people are then invited to pair off, and to get into the canoes and paddle about practising going forward, stopping and going backwards. This takes about fifteen minutes for both half-groups to do. This is a reminder of last week's work.

A brief talk follows by the coach from a canoe in the baths, everyone else watching from the bath side. Make sure your course members keep warm if the baths are cool.

Describe the sphere of movement, and tackle turning move number one, that is the sweep turn. Describe it, and concentrate on the following points :

1. Keep the arm ruler-straight, throughout the movement.
2. Make sure the paddle sweeps wide, and not deep.
3. Keep your eye on the paddle in the water.

The group now practises sweep turns. Another fifteen minutes have passed.

Another brief demonstration, and show straight line move number two, the draw stroke. Concentrate on these points :

1. Keep the normal paddle grasp at all times. Do not reverse the hand.
2. The upper arm pushes in the desired direction of movement.
3. Ensure that the blade release is learned before any power is put on.

The group now practises draw strokes, and it is time to get out.

SESSION THREE

As before, this starts with under-and-over swimming, six lengths and then the two half-groups practise all the previous work, forward, stop, backwards; turning; draw stroke.

A brief demonstration follows of the so-called 'slap supports' Emphasise the following points :

1. Raise a sunk paddle by turning it edge-on and slicing upwards.
2. Keep the outer arm slightly flexed, almost straight.
3. Introduce the hip flick (see the following section on Rolling).

The two-half groups practise this, and you should be on the look out for capsizes. About thirty minutes have now passed.

At this point we introduce canoe polo. The swimmer to canoeist rescue is often useful here in order to save time (see chapter on survival and rescue). The game has its rules, but locally we do it as follows. Instead of targets we use a touch-down on the bath end, almost like rugby. The ball is usually a plastic football. With six canoes, we play three a side. The contestants start off by backing up to the ends of the bath, and the game is over when five minutes have passed, or when one side has scored three goals or tries. Both half-groups must take part, and it is very useful in training for the following reasons :

1. People begin to try hard and ignore balance fears.
2. Capsizes are frequent, and people learn to stay in the canoe and await rescue.
3. Some of the fun and vigour of canoeing begins to make its mark on the course members.
4. Ability with the paddle is achieved more quickly than any other way I know.
5. It's fun, anyway.

ROLLING TUITION IN THE BATHS
The human animal can breathe provided that the nose and mouth are free from any smothering material, such as water. One way to achieve this happy state of affairs when in a canoe is to keep it the right way up. However, the normal progression of skills from novice to expert generally goes as follows :

1. Novice. Capsizes in calm water and on rough water.
2. Improver. Capsizes on rough water, usually stays upright on calm water.
3. Learns to roll sometimes on calm water. Improved stability in rough.
4. Rolls every time on calm water, rolls most times on rough.
5. Never capsizes in calm water, rolls every time on rough.
6. Rolls by many methods in practice, including hand rolling.

7. Simply never rolls because he always retains balance whatever the conditions.

Some places put their embryo-canoeists straight away into the swimming pool, where they learn to roll before learning to paddle. Then, whatever mistake they may make, they can always roll up and carry on – and thus not waste a great deal of time.

I know a happy man, George, who would roll his canoe wherever and whatever he was doing. I've seen him roll in less than a foot of water, he was so good. Trouble, because he had learned to roll so efficiently so early in his canoeing career, he hadn't at that time learned his technical paddling strokes because he really didn't need to. But when it came to examination for the Senior Instructor Award he wasn't good enough, because he didn't know his ordinary paddling strokes well enough.

BATHS ROLLING COURSE, NOVICES

This normally takes four sessions for twelve people in six baths canoes. Every session begins with over-and-under practice, because a canoeist can never be too good a swimmer, and usually ends with a rousing ten minutes of canoe polo, when precept is put into practice. Apart from that the basic principles are as follow :

Explain the basic concepts of rolling. There are combinations of the following possibilities :

1. Down left, up right; down right, up left.
2. Leaning forward or leaning backwards.
3. With a paddle or without a paddle.
4. If with a paddle, using a long lever (put across) or short lever (screw).
5. If without a paddle, using a buoyancy aid, or hands, or even (and extremely rarely) simply using body flick, no hands.

The instructor then does a short demonstration of all these methods, or as many as he can manage. Then the basic method is explained.

The basic method used always to be the pawlata roll which has been in use since the early thirties; but since an article by A. J. Broadbent appeared in the magazine *Canoe-*

ing (August 1970) we have changed our approach considerably. You see, in a fast 'wipe-out' on surf, or on a river, the fast-moving canoe is to some extent relieved of the weight of the paddler as he turns over and his body enters the water. The drag of the water on his body makes him lie back quite naturally along the rear deck, as the canoe runs ahead over him. This then puts him in an excellent position for rolling by the lay-back method, which is quite opposite to the pawlata laid-forward method.

Hip Flick Drill

Therefore, the next stage is to put the pairs of paddlers to their baths canoes, and to get them to practise hip flick drill. In this the paddler has the spray deck properly adjusted; he sits alongside the baths rail, both hands on the rail, canoe parallel to the rail, and he leans his canoe over. Points to watch are :

1. Hands about fifteen inches apart on the rail, overhand grasp.
2. Forehead well down on to the rail, touching it if possible.
3. Take canoe off balance so it lies almost upside down.
4. Retaining position in cockpit, flick canoe back on to balance by using hip action only. *Keep the head down*!
5. Repeat rapidly, say ten repetitions each side. Then the partners change places.

It should be noted that this practice is usually better done keeping the face downwards and with a forward body lean. However, some people can quite effectively lie back along the rear deck, face upwards, and by using one hand only, that nearest to the rail, bring the canoe on and off balance. The free hand is used as a moving counter weight to assist the righting movement. If one lies backwards the following points should be noted.

1. Back of head touching rear deck.
2. If rail is on right, grasp rail with right hand.
3. Keeping head back all the time, tip over towards rail.
4. Left hand can be used to check roll.
5. Canoe should be almost completely upside down.
6. Fling the left arm over the upturned canoe, at the same

time using the hip flick to right the canoe. *Keep the head back*!

Whichever practice comes easier, try to progress to the second, as it is more effective in real situations.

SWIM-UP PRACTICE

At this point the canoeist can be shown that he can stay in the canoe and still take air, even without a paddle. The rail drill is used, and then, after the paddler has accustomed himself to the rail, he capsizes and releases his grasp on the rail, having then to reach up and grab the rail before coming upright again. A sort of dog-paddle action when laid back will achieve this. Next, the partner helps by moving the canoe a little further from the rail ready for each capsize, until the person in the canoe is swimming several feet to grab the rail ready for the hip flick righting action.

BUOYANCY BLOCK ROLL

The partner stands clear but near by ready to help. The paddler uses an inflated lifejacket, which gives about 40 lb. effective buoyancy. Hip flick righting of the canoe is really quite easy for almost everyone using the inflated lifejacket. The lifejacket is then deflated and the drill repeated. Ensure, of course, that the valve cap is firmly in place on the lifejacket, or it can leak. This reduced buoyance, about 15–20 lb., is just about enough for the canoeist to obtain the lift he needs for his hip flick. At this stage improvement of the hip flick drill becomes essential, i.e. the head *must* be kept low, the flick must be energetic and quick, and the timing of the arm thrust and hip flick must be more precise. Finally the lifejacket is exchanged for the average baths float, and this gives quite enough support for the canoeist to come upright, if :

1. His head is low;
2. His flick is quick; and
3. His timing is right.

ROLL ON THE FLOAT

By now the canoeist will be leaning well back when coming

up, or leaning well forward. The lay back position is better in fact but some people work better laid forward and this does work just as well at this stage. Canoeist clasps the float in both hands in front of the chest, then works as follows. (Assuming that the previous practices have all taken place on the right-hand side.)

1. Lay back. Reach overhead and backwards with the float, over the left shoulder.
2. Head touching rear deck. Capsize, down left.
3. Swing under canoe, face downwards; keep swinging float towards left.
4. Reach up for surface with float. Head well back.
5. Thrust down on float, as in earlier practice.
6. Hip flick. Left arm swings over rear of canoe. Right hand grasps float.
7. Sit up, right hand deep in water holding float on right side.

PADDLE DRILL ONE, HALF ROLL
Assuming that the foregoing drills have been effectively learned, and that the last exercise, rolling up on the float, is working most times, then the paddle is used, as follows:

1. Grasp paddle in normal hold.
2. Partner takes right paddle tip in hands, and supports it.
3. Canoeist half rolls up on the shaft, repeating hip flick drill.
4. Canoeist then places blade where partner was but is no more.
5. He falls over on to the blade, and regains balance by thrusting against the resistance of the water on the paddle blade. This is much less solid in feel, unless done very quickly before water has time to spill away from the blade face.

PADDLE DRILL TWO, FULL ROLL
The canoeist sits normally in his canoe. He has practised paddle drill one and is usually successful with it. All he must do now is to go over on the side away from which he is to come up, and this introduces the slight confusion of sorting

oneself out under water when coming round underneath the canoe.

The following drill is for those who have been practising laid forward. It is a variant of the pawlata roll and is called the storm roll by some :

1. Paddle in normal paddling grasp.
2. Lay paddle along left side deck, right blade by left bow deck.
3. Drive face of blade turned upwards and inwards at about 45 degrees.
4. Head tucked forward in crook of right elbow.
5. Roll over left side down.
6. Sweep blade up towards water surface.
7. Swing blade away from canoe, straightening right arm, pushing with left arm.
8. Roll up as before, head low.
9. Sit up. Right paddle blade should be deep in water on right side, drive face turned in towards the canoe.

The alternative drill is for those who have been practising laid back along the rear deck, which is the better method when the roll in the rough is required :

1. Grasp paddle in normal grasp.
2. Line up paddle on foredeck as for the forward laid roll.
3. Raise forward paddle blade into air, turning it so that the drive face is turned inwards.
4. The right-hand blade is now swung backwards over the left shoulder and the left-hand blade is pointing forward and downwards on the left side.
5. The right arm is crooked over the head, and to do this the body must be turned to the left.
6. Continue the shoulder rotation thus begun towards the left, and capsize down left, looking backwards over the left shoulder, the head being braced back on to the rear deck, and placing right blade against rear deck near stern of canoe.
7. Continue the swing of the right blade in the same rotation under the canoe, swing it up towards the surface, on the far side.
8. Roll up on the paddle pressure as before (No. 7 above).
9. Sit up. The paddle blade should have moved forward on

the right side and be quite deep in the water, drive face toward canoe.

Hand Roll

This is really very simple. One continues the drills from the roll on the baths float, using progressively smaller floats, until the palm of the hand is enough.

Rolling Development

It frequently happens that one fails repeatedly. Don't continue vainly chasing the thing you can't do, that is, practising failure. Do go back to the part of the drill you know you can do very well, and build up from there again, practising success. I have known people, having had a nasty experience, go right back to the capsize drill, and then, as confidence is regained, build up very rapidly again to rolling successfully.

Once one has become successful in rolling in the calm and warmth of the baths, try rolling in a still part of a river on a warm day. Or, if one is by the sea, find a rock pool and practise in that. Then, on the river, find a fast-moving stretch with little waves on it, and cut across the stream, capsizing upstream, and rolling up downstream. On the sea one finds an area of small, two-foot waves, and capsizes towards the shore when lying parallel to the waves, just as a wave comes up abeam. Roll up on the seaward side. Practise and practise, frequently. Then go out in the big waves, or on to the really rough rivers and horribly boily weir races, and try your luck there. The sheer exhilaration of a flick roll on the face of a curling six-foot wave is hard to beat; it is almost instantaneous.

CHAPTER ELEVEN

Simple Challenges

Of course, it all depends what you mean by simple. As an expert rock climber once said to me as he showed me a vertical slab of rock sixty feet high with no apparent hold bigger than a match head, 'to me that's difficult, but you'd call it impossible'. And in canoeing, the last few years have produced a number of possibilities that once would have been classed impossible.

TWO-MAN RAFT CHANGE PLACES
1. Two people, each in his own canoe, (and preferably with leg lengths similar, or the canoes without footrests), face opposite ways and come alongside each other. Remove the spray decks.
2. Place the paddles across the canoes, each one behind the back of the paddler.
3. Place one hand on the centre of the cockpit at rear, one hand on the paddle shaft between the canoes.
4. Lift up behind and sit on the paddle shaft, a little towards the other canoe.
5. Swing feet across into other canoe, moving together.
6. One stands up, turns round, sits down.
7. Other stands up, turns round, sits down.
8. Settle into other canoe.

A group of novices, especially lively youngsters, find this a great deal of fun. It can be done in very shallow water or in very deep water, it doesn't matter much.

Two-Man Raft, Stand Up Sit Down

1. Two people each in his own canoe, spray decks removed.
2. Lie alongside, facing opposite ways.
3. One person lies across the foredeck of the other canoe, ensuring that the chest is pressed on to the deck, and the arm reaches right across and over the far gunwale of the other canoe. The other hand grasps the centre front of the other cockpit. Take care, as the spray deck is off, that the water doesn't come in.
4. The person in the canoe that is being held stands up, turns round, and sits down.
5. They then change roles and the other one does it.

This is a bit of fun for a novice group not more than twenty minutes on the water, and it is very good practice for the rescue systems which rely on two-canoe rafts for stability whilst one climbs in. Incidentally, this can be extended on warm days with warm water, the person standing up simply steps overboard, swims around the two canoes, and climbs back in again over the side. This can be made into a timed competition in a group of pairs.

Canoe Boots

One or more people take part. Each has a paddle and two canoes. These could be small baths boats. Stand with one foot in each boat, like enormous boots. Cause the canoes to move by adroit use of the paddle as a single-bladed device between the feet. The 'bootamaran' can be turned and moved backwards, and the paddle blade must remain under water all the time between the canoes. It is not easy, but an intelligent person will find ways of making the assembly move quite effectively. A neat way out of the situation, although a wet one, is to lay the paddle across the foredecks, and then do an overarm-swing-cum-handstand on the shaft, and thus swing over into the water in front of the two canoes. Arch the back so as not to hit the water flat on the back, a painful action; or curl up into a ball.

It is also possible for other canoeists to pass between the two canoes under the arched legs of the lunatic with the big feet, making a sort of slalom course with moveable gates and real penalties for the 'gates' if the paddler strikes them with either boat, body or paddle.

WIGGLE-WRIGGLE FOR NOVICES

The wiggle-wriggle standard gate, known as the English Gate in the States, is useful in order to improve the skill of novices.

The method is explained on p.142. However, the rules clearly state that there shall be no touch at all during the competition, and novices cannot manage that standard straight off. Therefore, run a timed competition, but for each touch of the poles add ten seconds to the time elapsed from start to finish. This is a useful idea, and the competitive urge in most young people will drive them on to do better next time. Keep a simple paper record on a clip board. You need a second hand on your watch, but a top-class stopwatch is not essential, as at this level a two-or three-second latitude in timing is quite acceptable with scores up in the three-or four-hundred-second bracket with penalties. Anyone scoring less than two hundred first time out is either very lucky, or perhaps very good.

MINI LONG DISTANCE RACE

A proper long distance race is over ten miles for seniors and over seven miles for juniors and ladies. However, when novices gather together with a handy five-kilometre circuit nearby with two portages, or one weir shoot and one portage depending on how it is tackled, then a shorter race is a good thing. Keep times, of course, and have someone reliable, preferably a lifesaver and canoeist, standing by at the weirs keeping an eye on things. We found that six youngsters about fourteen managed to get round in anything from thirty-five minutes to an hour and a bit. The keen youngster will take the shoot at full blast, but only if he has been coached over it beforehand. One must know one's charges to be able to do this with reasonable safety. It is really amazing how a fast portage with another youngster close behind will improve a youngster's time at a portage from nearly ten minutes to less than two.

THE SEAL LAUNCH

This can be done endways or sideways. If the surface is a slippery slope into the water with no sharply defined edges, then go endways. On a hard surface, say a timber jetty or a concrete embankment, go off sideways.

A variation is to use a ladder, and tip the boat over the edge using the ladder as a tilting slipway. This is done endways.

Endways: Select a suitable bank, grassy and wet perhaps, or wet mud. Be sure that there is enough water to drop into, because if the bows stick in shallow mud, and the other end is still up on the bank you will 'spindle over' and find yourself in a capsize with the cockpit about two feet above the water – and that can be nasty.

Make sure that the canoe won't set off when one is halfway into the cockpit, even though this is great fun for the people watching.

Preferably be just above the beginning of the steep slope. When full settled into the canoe, spray deck on, paddle in hand, use the paddle as a pole and push off down the slope, to gather speed and plunge into the water. The bows slide deeply through the water then rise. Water rises to the cockpit. A total drop of about four feet is good to begin with. I've seen lads beside the bridge by the Centre come whizzing down a forty-foot slope with a vertical height of twenty feet without harm.

Sideways: The jetty edge can be about two feet high to begin with, but I've seen a big man jump off sideways from the harbourmaster's jetty at Cowes, and that must have been a six-foot vertical drop. He did make a big splash – to the accompaniment of nasty crunching noises from where the seat was attached to the deck.

Get into the canoe, with one side of the canoe overhanging the drop. Provided that not more than half the width of the canoe overhangs, and that on entering the canoe one leans slightly toward the land side, all will be well.

Put on the spray deck, etc., and with paddle in hand and a great shuffle of the bottom, to which the canoe is attached, go sideways into the water, leaning a little towards the water and driving the paddle deep and away from the landing on which to do a support on a vertical shaft.

It's spectacular, it grabs the attention of a group of school-boys waiting for 'Sir' to take to the water, and it very rapidly renders the canoe a spongy heap of old fragments of G.R.P. material.

SEAL LAUNCH

END-ON: SOFT EDGE // SIDEWAYS: HARD EDGE

But it is not a silly, unnecessary bit of showing-off entirely. I had to get off a ledge on the Great Orme once during a force six wind into a weltering sea, and that was the only way. I had to time the jump as the crest surged up to the edge of the ledge, and to go like a bat out of Hell before the next wave washed me back again into the craggy rock.

RESCUE RACES

Divide the party into groups of two, or three, or four, provided they all have the same number in them. Send them off in a mass-start to some point, where they must leap out of their canoes, run around the land-based mark, and return in their canoes to the starting point. However, on the way everyone of each group must take part as a patient in a deep-water rescue. The winning group is that which has all its soaking wet members back at the start first, complete with boats.

Offer a prize, and it doesn't half make them go!

WEIR SHOOT AND OBSTACLE RACE

The weir is running, and it must be a suitable weir for shooting. If you try to do it when the weir is unsafe, then you could end up very dead.* However, if the weir is a suitable one, then there is fun to be had. Most weirs have a spillway, and then gates of two kinds nearby. The gates on the Thames are either butts, which move straight up and down in big frames, or radials, which hinge about a great pivot, and being balanced can be swung up by a man using a key on a geared bevel. In both cases the water rushes out below the gate, and causes a big boil-up with a possible return flow, especially in the case of the radial. The butt weir may usually be lifted completely clear of the water, and a solid spout of water rushes through and causes a large standing wave, but there is not very often a return flow on this, and it tends to be less dangerous than the radial weir.

If the spill is running, but the gates are all closed, it is possible to shoot the weir (although usually against the bye-laws) and then to paddle around in the turmoil by the spout of water running from the spillway. To avoid a difficult or long portage around the weir, possibly over someone's private land, discover ways of climbing over the top of the closed weir gates. Check the water depth below the gate. It can often be only a foot or two deep, in which case it's easy to step out, lift the canoe over the gate, and then re-enter above the weir.

There are dangers with weirs, that are not always obvious. In one, not a thousand miles from Durham Cathedral, there is a side gate with a metal grill just above the weir on the

*NB. In advocating this form of exercise, the author could be accused of irresponsibility. However, if one is thoroughly to understand what water can do, a close involvement is essential. It's fun, too, and it helps to satisfy that 'Ulysses Factor'. It is surely better that adventurous youth should find satisfaction in this way rather than in offering violence to others. Nevertheless, a do-it-yourself approach to this entertaining side-line of canoeing can lead to difficulties if the weir and the water are not thoroughly understood by someone in the party; and that usually implies an older person who has lived long enough to see many weirs, and to know which are possible, and which are not, and in particular one who *knows* the weir to be used, from the canoeist's point of view.

right-hand side going downstream. If one should be in the water here, it would be quite easy to be pulled against the grill by the flow of water, and to be very firmly held there. If one should be under water at the time, which is not impossible, then drowning would be quite likely.

Returning to the Thames weirs, if a butt gate is slightly lifted, as can happen if some obstruction down below props the gate up from the bottom, then there is a powerful but small flow of water under the bottom of the gate, to be discerned by seeing the water below the apparently closed gates boiling up continuously. If one should fall into the water above the weir it is not impossible to be drawn down to the bottom of the gate and then jammed there, helpless.

Weirs are fun, *but for everyone's sake, know your weir before you try any tricks with it!*

Under the Low Bridge

Near the Centre we have several low farm bridges over a stream. I call one of these trips the 'Dirty Ditch Safari', and you'd know why if you'd been on it. Soon after branching off the Thames just by the University Boathouse one comes to a very low bridge over the stream. The headroom is about twenty inches, the depth about two feet. Various alternative ways of passing the bridge exist. You could of course portage, but that is cheating. Given confidence, try the following:

1. Take the paddle shaft in a firm grasp, right-handed for right-handers, but the surroundings may alter this choice, and place the complete paddle flat on the bottom on the right side. It will be necessary to lean right over to do this, perhaps off balance. Reach overhead with the left hand, and with the eyes and ears and nose and mouth turned up to the air, shuffle along the shaft, and by pressing upwards on the left hand pull and thrust the way completely under the bridge.

2. If the water is too deep for that, have the group work in pairs, and one person goes right up to the bridge so that the chest is pressed up to it. The partner then comes alongside and leans across on to the foredeck of the upright canoe. The canoe to go under the bridge then is pulled by its paddler and pushed by his partner until he has traversed the length

of the assistant's canoe, and should then be free to pop up on the other side. If he isn't far enough through, then the

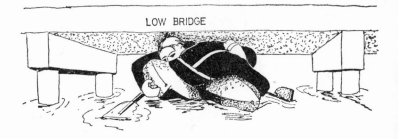

LOW BRIDGE

assistant may lean over on to his partners rear deck, and the pair, leaning on each other's canoes, may then drift through, catamaran fashion.

This method could have averted a near disaster on a flooded river on one occasion. The river runs from Llyn Padarn to Caernarvon in North Wales. It drops about three hundred feet in seven miles, and a basic description of a white water river is a drop of fifty feet per mile. One day, with a high flood running, two expert canoeists set off on this great little river. Belting along at full tilt, about ten m.p.h. over the land, and whizzing past rocks and trees and bushes, they came upon a low bridge, head room just about zero, and being apart and surprised, they simply had to capsize to avoid being brained.

The bridge had a gate hung on the far side to slow down rubbish floating on the river, and this knocked them out of their canoes. One came up in a back eddy under the bridge, and all he could see was his canoe vanishing at a great rate down the river. His partner was nowhere to be seen. Sadly he climbed out and then ran like blazes to a nearby farm for help and search teams. His partner had been swept on around the bend and on making his way back, had seen his own canoe and that of *his* partner go flashing by on the flood. He too ran for help. They met at the farm. Perhaps, if they had been able, they could have leaned on each other's canoe and thus hurtled under the bridge with the minimum of clearance . . . but maybe not. Its easy to be philosophical about another man's misfortunes.

THE CATERPILLAR

It's a fine calm day, and you are pottering about on the river wondering what to do next. Select a partner. Ensure that the spray decks are on firmly and the end loops on the canoes, and that the canoes are of about the same foredeck length. Put down your paddles.

Grasp the end loop of the canoe opposite you (it must be facing the opposite way), and your partner does the same with your canoe.

Take a deep breath, and lie across the foredeck and bows of the opposite canoe. Your partner sits upright.

Dive headfirst over the other canoe and, as you slide under the water, your canoe slides over the foredeck of the other canoe, and your partner heaves your bows across his foredeck.

You are now upside down and wondering what has happened, but do the natural thing, simply pull on the end loop of the other canoe and you should pop up in an Eskimo rescue.

Straight away your partner does the same thing over your bows, and you help him across. Frequently repeated the sight is ludicrous and very entertaining, apart from being good Eskimo rescue practice. Failure is usual at first, but persevere.

ROCK DODGING

This is not simple, and it can be a boat wrecker. First one requires a cliff with rocks in the water below it, big rocks – maybe reefs with water channels between.

The canoeist should be in a fully kitted-out slalom kayak, complete with all equipment including crash helmet, and he should be very able in manoeuvring and clever paddling strokes certainly of advanced standard.

The group waits near to some rocks, on the open sea side, taking care not to be washed into the rocks prematurely. A suitable gap in the rocks is selected, preferably wider than the length of the longest canoe in the group. A narrow gap would be a source of trouble, as a canoe becoming jammed across the gap would be subject to the full press of water as a wave surged through, and could break into halves.

Running these gaps, as the waves surge through, is exciting. The wave height is enhanced by the narrowing of the gap, and so increased speed and carrying power of the wave is felt. On a calm day this can offer fun for the group.

Being satisfied that the next set of waves is not too large to handle, ease the canoe forward into the gap between the rocks, and feel the lift and surge as the wave heaves forward and under the canoe. Because of the venturi effect of the gap in the rocks the waves peak up and gain forward speed, so that one can surf through. If the gap is not very long, the trough of the wave will not pass by. But if it does, then the next thing is that the crest of the same wave which has gone the long way round the rocks comes surging back up the gap, thus presenting a head-on collision with white water.

It's great fun, but keep paddling.

Also, but strictly for experienced paddlers, is rock dodging, playing follow-my-leader. You can find fun on a calm day doing this.

You may wonder, having read this chapter, what use could these stunts possibly have? Swapping places, sliding off mud banks, standing up in two canoes: here we have reasonable people cavorting about doing what may seem to be silly things just because this book suggests them as being good ideas?

Stunts are fun, and enhance handling ability in a canoe. What is a stunt on, say, the calm waters of the Thames, may become a very useful way out of a difficult situation on a sea cliff, or on a muddy estuary. In addition flexibility of body and mind are improved. The old saying 'There are more ways of killing a cat than stuffing it with cream' is applicable here. Practice stunts in canoes, and you will start to develop a flexible approach to canoeing which can be of great assistance on many occasions.

Please do not reject them out of hand, unless, perhaps, you are a solo canoeist, and so unable to practise some of these actions, or not a youngster, for I must confess that much of this book is written with younger people in mind.

CHAPTER TWELVE

Rescue and Survival

Survival implies a determination to keep a strong hold on life. Survival is equipment properly used. Survival is knowing enough to minimise the adverse affects of a situation. Avoidance of bad situations is often possible by advance planning, but sometimes when exploring the limits of one's previous experience one finds a survival situation developing.

The bodily aspects of survival will be dealt with in this chapter, but one must first have this in mind, that survival is of the whole person, therefore charge one's spirit with resolve to endure and survive. That decision made now, possibly in the comfort of one's own chair in a warm room in calm conditions, is the precondition for survival when the difficulties crowd in and danger is real and present, and there are no reserves of skill or resources except that will to go on.

Rescue implies that others must come to the aid of the person in difficulties. There may be more than one of either. Implicit in the relationship that develops between the rescuer(s) and rescued during the act of rescue is some degree of risk of failure; and, depending on the nature of the method of rescue used, then the risk may be shared, or placed more upon the rescued or more upon the rescuer. Until one has some experience of various types of rescue in different conditions, mostly practice, with a few real rescues encountered along the way, then one is unable to discriminate between one method and the other, and whether the burden of risk should be placed on one person more than on another. At novice level it is not necessary to know the methods available before going canoeing; however, *before* one tackles enterprising canoeing such as the Irish Sea crossing or the cliffs of Anglesey, or perhaps the intricacies of the tidal surges around the Farnes, one should be reasonably proficient on a river, and that sort of work begins when the novice first rafts up with his partners, and maybe tries the two-man raft on his first session.

Remember if it were necessary to know everything before attempting anything, nothing would be done. So risk is involved. I hope that the risks you will encounter when canoeing may be reduced by knowledge and lessened by progressive experience. Plus a little luck.

This reminds me of a reassuring comment heard from a skilled canoeing coach in the past: ' 's all right kid', he said 'life's a fatal experience anyway! Enjoy what you've got left!'

On another occasion, a group was crossing from the mainland to Cowes, Isle of Wight. A youth among the group gifted with a vivid imagination was clearly very worried . . . 'gripped' in the parlance of the outdoor schools. The instructor noticed this, and to cheer him up pointed out the ferry trundling across the rather choppy waters over the Bramble Bank towards Cowes.

'See that son?' he said. 'It's five hundred times more dangerous than your canoe. You, see, there must be five hundred people aboard, and so if it sinks, maybe five hundred people would drown. Now, if *you* go down, there'd only be one to drown, now wouldn't there?'

EXPOSURE
This really means hypothermia, or excessive cooling of the body so that the body temperature drops to a level where life can no longer continue. You get so cold that your heart stops beating. But before that the body goes through several fairly distinctive stages, and the first of these is often experienced by canoeists. Briefly the stages are four, and the rate at which one moves through one into the next is governed chiefly by the rate at which body heat is lost, but

the effects of this on the person are not accurately predictable, as imponderables such as spirit and experience and the will to live are involved. The four stages are :

1. Cooling of the extremities.
2. Inability to control the limbs.
3. Loss of consciousness.
4. Coma and death.

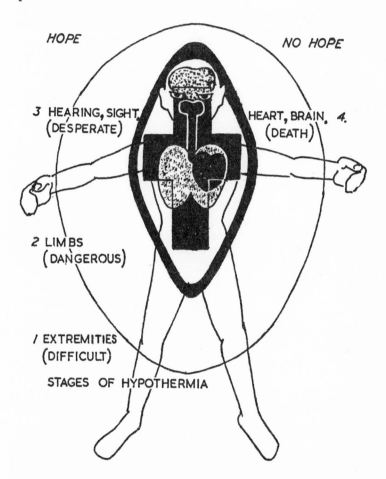

Stage One: When the extremities are cooled, the hands become painful, but may soon become tolerably warm as the body adjusts to the demands of the cooled hands. The feet become cold, and the nose and ears and face become chilled, painfully so. Shivering begins as the body begins to feel the lowering of temperature generally and so builds up heat by muscular agitation, and this can be quite exhausting. If the cooling goes on a long time, frostbite may result, even in temperatures just around freezing. The skin tissues exposed to the cooling air simply die, and the dead skin becomes a scar tissue on the face or hands. It is a very difficult condition to remedy without permanent scarring.

Stage Two: By this time one is likely to have become quite afraid, and a sense of anxiety is very strong. It is at this point that determination to keep on going will assist in survival. One goes through the barrier of fear, and learns to accept that if the cooling goes on then there is only a limited time left in which to continue actively to make survival attempts. The limbs lose the sensation of cold quite quickly, a continuing sense of cold is not much in evidence, but a numbness of the limbs is noticeable. Hearing soon becomes affected, and the movements of the limbs are slowed and laborious, or cease quite suddenly. Sight is affected and balance is altered. Vision becomes blurred; hearing is dulled, and sounds become far away and dream-like. Anxiety does not usually continue after the start of this stage.

Stage Three: In stage two attempts at communication have been becoming more difficult, and in stage three it is impossible to rouse the person to reply to questions, or to produce more than a mumble from him. The victim is possibly on the edge of being lost; he needs skilled medical help, and all he has is you, on some freezing river bank, or on some remote clump of boulders under a sea cliff. This person is possibly a dead one if *you* don't act at once.

Stage Four: The body's temperature balance is controlled by the autonomic nervous system, which works quite automatically at normal body temperatures. In extremely cold conditions, the system is impaired, and loses its control. The very cold surface blood invades the core blood supply and there is a fatal collapse. This state is sudden, and some people have been known to go from stage three back to stage two as they begin to recover, and then they slip into stage four in a state of shock and die in a minute or two.

This of course is a layman's interpretation of a very complicated physical and psychological balance; but I have been to the indistinct boundary between stage two and stage three and recovered, so I feel I can write with some authority on this business. Doctor Pugh wrote an article in the *British Medical Journal* in January 1966 which recorded many accidents. It was entitled 'Accidental Hypothermia in Campers, Climbers and Walkers'.

ACTION TO BE TAKEN

I suppose laymen are regarded with some doubt by the medical profession, and believe me I wouldn't want my appendix removed by an enthusiastic amateur...but remember friend, you may be the only person present as your companion sinks through the stages of exposure, and what indeed can you do about it?

Briefly, the following:
1. Identify the condition.
2. Stop the loss of heat.
3. Start a gain in heat.
4. Keep the patient still and quiet until he is warm all over.
5. Report to the Doctor.

In stages one and two the victim will be able to recover without the intervention of others. If he has progressed into stage three, active help from his companions will be necessary. The first priority is to make the victim comfortable; the next is to obtain medical help if at all possible.

The paddler of the canoe becomes tired. His paddling action droops down, he flattens out. He looks tired, and complains of cold, probably also of hunger and weariness. However he may wish to cover up these signs of weakness, so he may talk animatedly, and become excitable, and have short bursts of energy which quickly lapse. He may cease paddling, and request a tow. He looks worried, and may start worrying audibly. Give him food, let him rest a few minutes, by rafting with him if necessary, talk to him. Feed him hot sweet drink from a flask (but beware of the unpredictable effects of alcohol, which helps some and hinders others). Check his clothing and ensure that it is drawn closely about the neck and head, and that it is windproof. If it isn't, give him anything available to cover the neck and head. It must be windproof to be effective.

2. If the victim has gone into stage two, he may need a tow, and you should go ashore if at all possible.

It will be necessary to consider abandoning the expedition, bearing in mind the alternative ways in which one can regain the comfort of shelter quickly as possible. Get the victim ashore, and put him in an exposure bag and get in with him. Strip off his wet clothes *only* if you can replace them at once with dry clothing. His clothing does two things, even when wet : in still air it prevents heat from being lost outwards from his body; and it also prevents heat from being received inwards towards his body. One idea, therefore, is for both rescuer and patient to strip right off, so that heat transfer between the fitter and warmer rescuer is not reduced by layers of soggy cold clothing. You may have to overcome some prudery at this stage, but make up your mind now about that. Save a life or blushes?

However enthusiastic stripping is not recommended at the commencement of stage two. Feed the person hot drink and food, like chocolate. Self-heating cans of soup are rather difficult to obtain, but very useful in this situation. The victim should recover fairly easily from this stage. As he warms up he will start to shiver violently until he is really warm again, but this is very exhausting, and so further heavy physical effort that day must be avoided and every help given, even though the victim may feel very well when warm again. It is almost certain to be necessary to abandon the expedition, and take the quickest possible means to get home or back to base.

3. If stage three is reached, it will be necessary to get heat into the victim's body soon, either by warming him with your own body heat, body close against his body, or by warm drinks

if he is conscious enough to take them, or both if the weather and surroundings are cold. As the victim comes back to life, he will go back through stage two, and that is when you should weigh up the chances of getting outside assistance. The warming up may be very slow, however, and the victim could still collapse and die.

4. If he is in stage four, do your best to warm him and maybe use artificial respiration and chest massage. Keep his head low to allow the brain to receive as much of the sluggish blood flow as it can get. Incidentally it is a good idea to keep the head lower than the feet at all stages unless actually feeding him, and to insulate the body from cold ground by putting something underneath him Try to get medical aid, *somehow!*

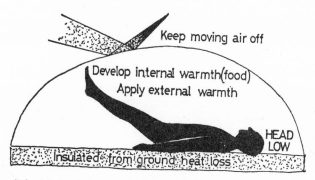

Keep moving air off

Develop internal warmth(food)
Apply external warmth

HEAD LOW

Insulated from ground heat loss

Principles of treatment of exposure

CLOTHING

The novice will begin with what he can, and the aims should be as follow :

1. Keep the body covered and windproof.
2. Keep the head covered and clothing around the neck drawn close.
3. Wear gloves.
4. Use a spray deck, as the part of the body under the deck is out of the wind, and therefore quite warm. If he comes

out of his canoe put him back in again as soon as possible, its warmer there.

Simple clothing can be : Swimming things and plimsolls (basic); a close fitting cotton shirt, like a rugby shirt; an old plastic mac, with elastic bands at the wrists, but not tight; a woollen cap; something to keep the neck covered, say a rolled towel tucked in like a scarf.

If there isn't an old plastic mac, get a plastic sack as used for fertiliser by farmers, and tear a hole at each corner for the arms, and a hole for the head, and wrap up with a towel inside that.

Gloves should be loose fitting and waterproof. A pair of easy fitting kitchen gloves do very well. If they are tight, then the hands will become painful, and very cold. A pair of silk or thin cotton gloves under the outer gloves will keep the hands warm.

The cost of the necessary clothing can vary from almost nothing to over fifty pounds, but it depends on what you want to do and where and when you do it. I use a Bukflex overall suit with a windproof nylon anorak over it, neoprene gloves, and divers' boots with tough soles. On my head I wear an old army wollen cap. My suit of canoeing clothes cost me about twenty pounds altogether. Frankly, I retire to the work-shop at winter time and avoid cold-weather canoeing as much as possible. Well, I do it for fun, so why make it painful?

Finally, in considering protective clothing, remember that it is the wind that causes the apparent temperature to drop alarmingly. The wet body in still air will survive quite well, but in an air-flow as little as six m.p.h. the rate of heat loss is so great from a naked wet body that serious exposure would follow in very little time. There is a great deal of technical know-how in this aspect of canoeing, so if you want to know more, join a canoe club; ask the British Canoe Union for advice. The address is at the back of the book.

RESCUE METHODS

There are several different types of rescue which are basic, and each basic method can be adapted in many different ways to each situation as it develops. However, it is enough to outline three methods and recommend that you try these out. They can be fun to practise, and when you can do these easily, then other ideas will be obvious and available if needed.

The people involved are the victim – the person in the water – and the rescuers, numbers one to whatever number there are available.

The effort of lifting the canoe out of the water in order to empty it, and then to lift the person back into the canoe may be too great for the victim to manage himself. This effort may be shared among several, or necessarily borne by one. The risk may be more upon the rescuer or the victim, depending on the method used or on the situation. If there is only one, or two rescuers, then the risk should be put upon the victim if at all possible, because if the only rescuer also becomes a victim, then you are both in real trouble.

If there are three or more rescuers around, then a rescuer may even take the place of the victim in the water when the emptying of the canoe is necessary, and the victim incapable of helping at all. The rescuer in the water then climbs back into his own canoe. Decisions on risks and who should carry them are the responsibility of the group leader. Party discipline and trust are very important in some cases, but the novice canoeist may not, or should not, be in such difficult situations from the beginning. The question of *not* attempting to rescue one, for fear of risking the many may even present itself.

METHOD ONE : SWIMMER TO CANOEIST

The canoeist is inverted and unable to breathe. Let it be assumed he is stunned – either with a blow, as in canoe polo, or with cold and weariness. He hangs upside down in the cockpit, locked in by pressure differences around the spray deck, and by the knee and thigh braces (but note that active canoeists can in fact swim up to the side, using what is a racing breast stroke action to lift the head above the water in order to draw breath).

A nearby swimmer, who can get there quickly, sets off at

a racing speed and swims straight across the inverted bottom of the canoe until his hips are tight up to the side of the boat, his chest laid across it, and he can reach down into the water on the far side of the canoe, there to seek and grasp the arm or shoulder of the victim. The rescuer then heaves backward in a lunging movement and hauls the victim upright. As he swings upright he is gaining momentum, and could continue straight over on top of the rescuer, and that is unwanted. To prevent this happening, just as the victim is coming up to the vertical, thrust back hard on the lifting arm. This prevents the victim from going over the top, and drives the rescuer down into the water.

This method is very useful in swimming pools, and as a confidence practice. It is also very useful for saving time which would otherwise be consumed by beginners having to leave an upturned canoe and empty it out, and then re-enter. Get them to stay in, and bring them up like this if they fall over. In this method the victim is in risk of drowning, but the whole effort of getting him upright is on the rescuer.

METHOD, TWO – THE 'X' METHOD

This involves a person who has come out of his canoe and left it floating upside down with very little water in it. The rescuer is wearing his spray deck and is alone and nearby. Note that this method is very difficult if there is a great deal of trapped water in the upturned canoe.

The rescuer takes charge. The victim swims to the bows of the rescuing canoe. He takes his paddle with him. The rescuer takes hold of one end of the upturned canoe and holds it near his cockpit. He must put down his own paddles to do this, and he can either hand them to the victim, or trap them under the deck line or elastic over the foredeck.

The rescuer then makes a powerful effort, and it must be quickly done. He lifts the end of the upturned canoe across his foredeck just in front of the cockpit (but beware: if the deck is weak it can crumple under the strain). The upturned canoe is then hauled very quickly across the foredeck until the front edge of the upturned cockpit rim is on the deck. The need for speed is in order to reduce the time when the rear or lower part of the cockpit rim is half out of the water, when air can escape from the canoe, and water spill in over the cockpit rim.

The further end of the upturned canoe is weighted down with water. On the sea the natural tilting of the canoes on the waves helps emptying out, provided that the effort is synchronised with the wave motion. On flat water it is necessary to rock the canoe across the foredeck. This can be done by the rescuer alone, who keeps on pulling the heavy

ROCK OUT

"X" RESCUE METHOD

end of the upturned canoe across his foredeck until it is so far across the foredeck that it becomes possible to rock it out.

It is possible to lean right out in this situation, as the end of the canoe across the foredeck acts as a very powerful outrigger and prevents capsize.

If the heavy end is too heavy, and if there is another

rescuer (No. 2) nearby, he can help by reaching down into the water at this point, and lifting the heavy end as the rescuer (No. 1) rocks it across his foredeck.

The victim is put back into the canoe by the normal two-man raft (page 133).

In my work as warden of the Riverside Centre in Oxford, it quite frequently happens that some person in my charge on the Thames tips out. It is then a matter of a quick sprint across to the incident, and by using the 'X' method I have the person back in his canoe in less than two minutes. This distracts my attention from the rest of the group, but for the minimum possible time. If we are trying something enterprising, such as break-in practice on a weir race, then there is a pre-arranged agreement that everything stops until I am free again. I suppose that of the many hundreds of rescues I have done, most have used this method.

METHOD THREE

The worst possible situation that the canoeist can encounter is the dreaded 'Cleopatra's Needle'. The canoe is non-buoyant at one end, and is almost always a G.R.P. canoe with the buoyancy bags, or blocks, or whatever, completely missing. This can be avoided by ensuring that *each* end of the canoe is fitted with effective buoyancy before setting off. The minimum effective buoyancy should be thirty pounds or half a cubic foot of polystyrene foam, *at each end*.

However, the worst has happened. The canoe has taken a great deal of water into it, and is riding vertically with the cockpit rim about a foot under water and the end of the canoe wagging about overhead, or at head level for the rescuers. The lower end will be about ten feet deep.

Two rescuers are required, and the person in the water must be active and strong. If the victim is weak, then there is a case for a third rescuer to raft up, get out of his canoe, and go into the water to take the place of the victim during the rescue. He gets back into his canoe after the rescue is complete.

The two rescuers raft up parallel, about two feet apart, and both facing the victim. The victim holds on to the bows of one of the rescuing canoes. His canoe is floating between the two rescuing canoes about level with their bows, and he hands his paddle to the rescuers. They place the three paddles across their foredecks. This – called the HI Method – makes a beam across which the victim's canoe can eventually be rocked out.

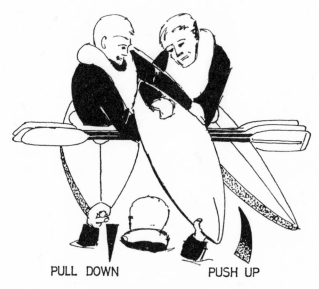

PULL DOWN   PUSH UP

"H.I." METHOD

The victim turns the vertical canoe so that the cockpit is towards him. He grips the cockpit rim with one hand, fingers under the rim, palm upwards. He grasps the bow of one of the rescuer's canoes. I find that, as a right-handed person, it is better as a victim to face the two rescuing canoes, left hand holding the left-hand bow as I face them, and right hand holding the cockpit rim as described, with thumb pointing away from the raft.

The victim then pushes the vertical canoe towards the rescuers' hands. They, or one of them, reaches up and grasps the upturned end, and pushes it down and *under* the paddle shafts across the canoes. The waterlogged canoe, if heavily waterlogged, may be surging with the entrapped water, so there may be a risk of the bows surging under and the ends changing places above the surface.

When the canoe is level, possibly with the cockpit opening turned upwards, the victim must ensure that part of the cockpit rim must be under water to allow entrapped water to flow out, and part of the rim must be above water to allow air to flow in to take the place of the outgoing water. At this point the victim is lifting quite powerfully, with his lifting arm doing a vertical thrust up from the shoulder. He may be pressing single-handed about thirty to fifty pounds, and he obtains the resistance to make the lift from pulling down on the rescuer's bow.

The rescuers, meanwhile, are holding the canoe end down, concentrating on keeping the victim's canoe level and correcting tilting due to water surge in the canoe. When about half the canoe has been lifted up in the water and about half the cockpit is showing, the rate at which the water flows out begins to slow down. The victim is finding lifting very difficult, even though he gets his power to lift from holding on to the rescuer's canoe. At this stage rest the canoe upright on the water, and take a breather. The victim will probably be panting with effort, but the rescuers are not much involved yet.

When ready to start again, the victim tilts the canoe towards him again, the cockpit opening turning over on to him, almost. At this moment the rescuers lift the end they have on to the paddle shafts, and pull hard, so that the canoe starts to slide in towards them. The victim releases his grasp on the cockpit rim and supports the moving canoe on the crook of his arm, trying, as the width of the canoe becomes less as it slides towards the rescuers, to get his shoulder under it. The rescuers will experience a little difficulty as the fore edge of the cockpit rim snags on the paddle shafts, but a little upward heave will free that. The victim is now supporting the waterlogged end of his canoe on his shoulder, the canoe is upside down over the paddle shafts, and rocking out may commence.

The rescuers lean back so as to get their weight as far

back as possible to counter the weight of the trapped water. The victim must make what can be a very severe effort if there is a lot of water in his canoe, and he lifts with a single arm press from the shoulder and thus starts the water moving towards the cockpit. The first part of the lift is the most difficult until the inertia of the trapped water is overcome. As soon as it starts to move and to pour out of the cockpit, the job is as good as done. A simple rocking out follows, the canoe is turned upright, and dropped down between the two rescuers. The victim then climbs back into his canoe, using the two-man raft method.

Re-entering a Canoe
Several methods of re-entering a canoe can be used. Many people prefer to have the two canoes parallel, in a two-man raft, both pointing the same way, and the paddles across the foredeck end of the cockpit. The victim lies between the two canoes, reaches up with his feet and hooks his heels over the paddle shafts, lies back in the water with his arms over the rear decks of the canoes, and humps his backside over into his cockpit. He then sits up.

I do not like this method, as the rescuer does not have a clear view of what is happening behind him on one side, and the efforts of the victim tend to push the canoes apart;

TWO MAN 'RAFT'

LAY ON DECK

Assisted re-entry

finally the rescuer cannot lend any support to the victim by grabbing his lifejacket straps, for example.

The better method in my experience is to have the two canoes facing opposite ways. The paddles are nearby but not necessary to the re-entry. The rescuer lies across on to the foredeck of the victims canoe. If it is on his right, he reaches over the canoe with his right arm and presses the palm of his hand underneath the canoe. His own canoe is tilted so that the spray deck is just under water on the right side. The right part of his chest is pressed hard down on to the foredeck, and his left hand grasps the centre front of the cockpit rim. Most of his upper body now lies across on to the victim's canoe.

The victim now comes to the offside of his canoe and holds the cockpit rim. He kicks his feet up behind him until they lie close to the surface. With a vigorous downward thrust on his legs and a quick hitch of the body over the cockpit rim, he should be lying across his cockpit, legs in the water, chin on the rescuer's spray deck. He can now wriggle down into the cockpit, or even, if he wishes, stand up and turn round.

I prefer this method because the victim is in full view of the rescuer; the efforts of the victim pull the two canoes together and help to stabilise the raft; the re-entry can begin without having to fetch the paddle first; and the rescuer can grab the victim by the scruff of the neck and haul him back into his canoe by sheer force if necessary. Finally the rescuer's body weight being laid on the patient's canoe does make the raft a very solid one with a rigid non-wobbling feel to it, and this assists confidence.

Other methods exist but these are specialist methods used by canoe rescue units when rescuing an unconscious swimmer, for example.

CHAPTER THIRTEEN

Competition

Canoeing, unlike football, does not require another twenty-
one people and a large, marked-out field, plus a high degree
of physical fitness, for one to enjoy it. However, some of the
most dedicated physical fitness fiends can be found in the
ranks of top-class canoeists in Britain. Look at it this way:
given a sports afternoon at a school, and there are two girls
left over from the netball, under thirteen, plus four enormous
sixteen-year-old spare rugby forwards, a student teacher doing
his practice and a games master wanting to occupy these
people. They can all go canoeing quite satisfactorily on the
local canal, river or pond, or even in the school pool.

However, competition is present in every human activity,
and develops to a greater or lesser degree. I offer the following analysis of competitive opportunities related to canoeing:

1. Man-man. I am better than you, I can go faster/further
than you.

2. Man-Nature. I can cope with natural difficulties more
efficiently than the next man.

3. Man-Himself. I can experience worse conditions than I
ever believed possible and retain my identity.

In category one above we have sprint races, long distance
races, canoe polo (I can score more goals than you can),
sailing canoe races, (I can understand the wind and weather
with a little more cunning than you can, and handle the
fastest single-hulled sailing boat in the world).

In category two come the white-water races, and slalom
events, and surfing competitions, where a degree of physical

ability plus a knowledge of natural phenomena plus a competitive urge combine to produce events of unusual complexity. This is the more commonly accepted description of competitive events. However, there is a separate branch in this category which relies more upon one's own difficulties in coping with natural phenomena, quite without any compression by artificial factors such as time, or gates, or courses.

Therefore in category two I include such things as deep sea canoeing, off cliff faces, in tide races, rock dodging under the cliffs, surfing for fun and surfing for necessity, playing with weirs and so on, always reaching out for more difficult experiences, without coming completely unstuck and fouling it all up with a drowning accident. This description fits category three, too. The distinctions are blurred.

In category three, there are soul-searching ways of appreciating canoeing, for example, the first capsize for a nervous novice; the appalling drop as a fifteen-foot dumper curls over just before the crunch on the beach at Bude, the endless series of curling standing waves in a tide race as one paddles on in despair that there can be any end to it, and yet eventually finding a quiet crevice in the cliffs away from it; and monstrous standing waves, well over ten feet high, with canoe-swallowing whorls on the Colorado. After this sort of canoeing one is never quite the same person one was before. Deep down inside, something changes, for ever, and who can say that the new 'you' is better or worse than before? You're just different, and you know it.

Another approach to competition in canoeing is to list the various known ways of canoeing competitively, and to give descriptions. For example :

1. Canoe Sprint.
2. Long-distance Racing.
3. Sailing canoe racing (Internation Canoe, ten square metres).
4. Surfing galas.
5. Canoe Polo.
6. Wiggle-Wriggle test.
7. White-water racing.

8. Canoe Slalom.
9. Record Breaking.

This is what we are doing at present. Ten years ago only half those competitions were in use. What will be taking place in another ten years is another matter.

CANOE SPRINT

Sprint canoes and kayaks are either solo, double- or four-place boats. Some of the very large Canadian ten-place boats have been used in competition on the Continent. The kayaks are mostly used in Britain, and these are usually made by Struer in Denmark from hot moulded veneers. The wooden sprint boat is a fraction faster than the identically shaped glass-fibre copy. The last I heard of prices for hot moulded wood laminates is that a K1 costs from £400 upwards, doubtless still rising as the pound plummets; a K2 costs somewhere about £600, and a K4 about a thousand. Glass copies have also risen but by nowhere near as much.

Sprint distances are 500 metres for junior events and ladies, 1,000 metres for international events, and 10,000 metres for the larger boats like the K4. Club evening training and sprint league courses may be as short as 200 metres, which makes it possible to introduce youngsters to the game on what are really unsuitable courses. Suitable courses would be long enough to include start and run-out; wide enough to allow a lateral separation of 10 metres; and deep enough, say 3 metres, to eliminate bottom interference drag. International sprint courses will be in lanes to ensure that interference between adjacent paddlers is reduced. Local events need a starter and a timekeeper, basically, plus 200 metres of straight river, and enthusiastic youngsters to attempt to stay in Espada-class racing kayaks. The new design 'Espada' class for youth racing in Britain should bring out the latent abilities of the many youngsters who now go in for slalom.

LONG-DISTANCE RACING

This depends on what you mean by long distance. Usually this is accepted as being a natural course with weirs, rapids and portages to be dealt with, plus the need to get from A to B in the minimum possible time. There are basic requirements for the courses, a junior and ladies course being 8 miles, and a senior course 12 miles. They can be longer, and the courses can run out of estuaries on to the sea.

Canoe handling standards are very high for the better paddlers, and a good appreciation of natural influences like currents and wind and weather and a knowledge of the course comes into it. Also, sadly, the cunning chopping-up and cutting-out and wash-hanging that goes on has reduced some paddlers to violence on other competitors' boats and persons. Stern-hung rudders must be used, as underhung K boat rudders would be wiped off on a shallow rapid; but these overhung rudders are very vulnerable to damage in collisions, whether accidental or deliberate.

Other long-distance races exist which are very popular, like the Liffey Descent in Dublin, the Arkansas River Race in the U.S.A., the Devizes-Westminster race at Easter in Great Britain, with many others in South Africa and Spain and other countries.

Locally, in Oxford, we sometimes have a 'Mini LD' for youngsters, young people who have never raced before, and we set them off on a 5 kilometre course, about 3½ miles. All that is needed is a starter and timekeeper, who can be the same person, plus a marshal at each of the two weirs to see them safely by. This is a useful way in which to begin in competition. As competition becomes keener, techniques other than canoeing can win races. And some of these techniques are 'dirty' ones.

SAILING CANOE RACING

This started in the nineteenth century and has been refined through the years, but basically the canoe is similar to what it was in the beginning. The rig is Bermudan, with a sliding board for balance. It is a solo boat, and the control of all the sheets and halliards and rudder must be possible from the far end of the sliding board. This is slid out to windward and is necessary to balance the boat against the very great pressure of air on the wing-like mainsail, which is heavily battened. When it goes about it does it very quickly, and all the controls must be passed to the other side as the board is flung out on the opposite tack. Begin to move too soon, and the boards digs in, and one flaps on to the outspread sail just before the water closes over; move too late, and the whole thing falls over and you swim out from under the clinging sail. An expert can drop the boat, and by standing on the centre board have it upright in about five seconds and be on his way, and not get more than his toes wet.

The racing takes place on the Thames, at Hayling Island, and at other places such as Grafham Water. The 'IC 10', as it is known, is an International class of boat and is sailed all over the world. So far the British lead, but the class is small, although growing slowly.

SURFING GALAS

Each September the British Canoe Union holds its annual surfing and lifesaving competition. This has recently been at Bude, where the local people make one very welcome. The surfing part of this was, apart from through-the-break-line-and-back type races, pre-eminently the style and showman-ship event of handling in the surf. But recently this has been altered by the introduction of surf shoes, so-called, derived from the Malibou board, which is fitted with a deck like a canoe and can be rolled in a wipe-out, unlike a surf board, which must be left to God and providence. These boats came to Britain from California about 1970, and some locally-designed surf shoes are now available.

The event is judged on style, and poise, sportsmanship, safety-mindedness, and spectacular innovations. The full-size canoe can be rolled and looped, and when balanced on end the skilled paddler can use air shots with his paddle blade, and pirouette in the breaking surf in a most graceful and spectacular fashion. The runs are mostly forward, and the loops also, but whoever can produce safe and controlled back-ward movements is on to a winning move. The difficulty in going backwards is that the natural spring of the legs is not present on impact, say with the bottom, and a nasty jarring bang under the kidneys is the result. Furthermore, one cannot easily see where one is going and collisions may result.

The judges, five in number, perch on nearby rocks and watch all this, and generally it takes fifteen minutes to assess the scene fully, for each heat of up to eight performers.

Canoe Polo

This game is played with a ball, and the only connection with canoeing is that the players are waterborne, in canoe-like boats. It is played five a side for seven minutes each way. The canoes must be between two and three metres long, and be between 50 and 60 centimetres wide. The ends must be rounded so as to reduce impact with each other or the bath tiles. The goals are targets hung facing each other, 20-30 metres apart, with the lower edge two metres from the water

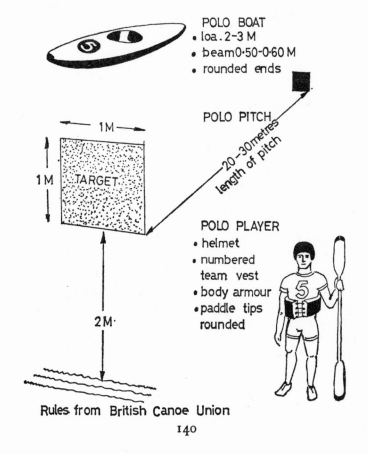

POLO BOAT
- loa. 2-3 M
- beam 0·50-0·60 M
- rounded ends

POLO PITCH
20-30 metres
length of pitch

1 M

1 M   TARGET

2 M·

POLO PLAYER
- helmet
- numbered team vest
- body armour
- paddle tips rounded

Rules from British Canoe Union

surface. The target is a one metre square. A goal is scored by striking the target with the ball, which is a standard plastic football. The paddles are used for propulsion and may be used for stopping the ball, as when defending the goal, but may not be used for striking the ball, as this is dangerous. Helmets are worn, also body armour to protect the spleen and kidneys from impact damage from fast-moving canoes. Paddle blades can be used like chopping axes, but this is dangerous play and the player can be set off, or even suspended until the governing body (which is the Polo sub-committee of the B.C.U. Competitions Committee) has decided the matter.

I played canoe polo on a lake in North Wales in 1960 under the refereeing of our Director of Coaching, Oliver Cock, and we used canvas canoes which were very rapidly reduced to splinters on impact, and so impact had to be penalised; but this is nigh impossible now, and with specialist boats in G.R.P. we can collide without much damage. The referee must decide what is dangerous play and what is not, and sometimes that can be very very difficult. Its not as if it were a football pitch where one can walk amongst the players!

Wiggle-Wriggle Test

Bill Horsman designed this system of standard training for gate practice in relation to slalom competition. His idea was that one could have club, regional, national and even international competition. At the very least one could compare one's own progress, matching times now with times past.

A simple, single gate is erected, under a bridge, from an overhanging bough or from a specially rigged gantry, or, best of all, across the width of a swimming pool in still water. The gate is four feet wide, the poles hang from a suspended horizontal support, with their inner vertical edges four feet apart, and with their lower ends about an inch above the water. the poles are about five feet long.

The timekeeper stands on the bank in line with the gate line, that is an imaginary line drawn across the water between the ends of the hanging poles. Timing starts when the bows of the canoe enter the gate line, and finishes when the stern ceases to break the line on the last gate. Novices can do it, with many bumps against the gate poles, and being talked through, in about three minutes. This time is quickly reduced to two minutes, and then, as the system is thoroughly learned, the test can be completed in just under one minute. It takes four or five attempts to reduce one's time by a minute from three minutes; it then takes about six months to reduce it to 70 seconds. Then, if one is very, very good, another year of experience can be spent in lowering the time to less than one minute.

THE WIGGLE GATE OR THE ENGLISH GATE
R = REVERSE

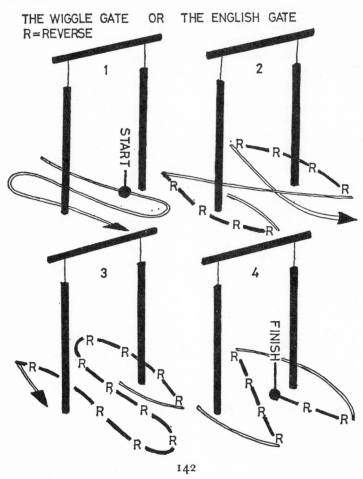

The test is divided into four parts, and these are shown as separate gates, but in fact the gate is the same gate used over and over again. There are three forward gates taken forward, two forward gates taken after reversing moves, two reverse gates taken in a reverse way, and two reverse gates taken after forward movements.

When talking people through I use the coaching words almost like a record. The trouble is, that to coach successfully in the this situation one must put oneself 'in the boat' alongside the paddler, and this way it is possible for the coach to get his right hand sorted out from his left hand; in other words, to refer your directions to the man in the canoe. Being, as it were, 'in the same boat', when the paddler makes a mistake, the frustration that one suffers is almost insupportable. So I apologise now for all the hard things I have said to earnest novices turning to the left when they should be going right. The words used are as follow :

'Left about means left shoulder to the gate, and so on.'
'Line up facing the gate, half a canoe's length away.'
'Forward through. Turn right about.'
'Forward through. Turn left about.'
'Forward through. Reverse past right.' (Roll in Wriggle).
'Forward through. Reverse past left.' (Roll in Wriggle).
'Forward through, reverse past left again, right about reverse turn.'
'Reverse through, left about reverse turn.'
'Reverse through, Forward past right.' (Roll in Wriggle).
'Reverse through, forward past left.' (Roll in Wriggle).
'Reverse through.'

Variations on the pure competition method (which requires no touches whatever, otherwise the run is void), include adding ten seconds to the time for each pole touched, however often, and this helps groups of novices who lack accuracy to gain it and do it in simple competition against the clock and each other. Also one can, if the paddlers are very good and turning in roughly equivalent times under seventy seconds, have scorers who count the number of strokes taken to do it, and so the time becomes less important and the need to develop fewer and more effective strokes is dominant.

I find this system very useful with novices. As with canoe polo, it encourages them to lean out in their canoes and transfer body weight on to the paddle blade and rely less on the natural balance of the canoe. It is a pressurising system which is very useful, to turn out confident boat handlers on smooth water and so pave the way for rough water skill.

The wriggle test is more demanding in that it requires a roll where specified, four in all, and this slows the time a little, but not very much. Experts will do the wiggle in 56 seconds, and the wriggle in 60 seconds.

WHITE-WATER RACING

Towards the end of the competitive season, around early October, organisers look for rivers which may offer plenty of rough water over a difficult course. There are no artificial hazards, but the natural hazards taken in conjunction with a race against the clock and against each other ensures plenty of excitement. Permission is obtained from landowners and angling societies, and the event takes place over the week-end. Typical courses are the upper Usk, the Tees, and the Dee at Llangollen. At this time of year, until early March in fact, rivers often have plenty of water in them, and anglers have off-seasons when their needs are not so demanding.

The race is a time trial. One favourite place is the River Leven white-water test, called the 'Dipper Test' A badge for proficiency is awarded and it is in the form of a tiny dipper, the bird that can run under water when fishing. It bobs its tail when perched on a rock. There are two standards for bronze awards, two standards for silver awards, and the gold award is for the fastest time of the year. On a typical week-end at the Lakeland campsite at Fell Foot on Windermere, about thirty able paddlers, skilled on grade three and more difficult water, will meet and run the one and a half miles of river maybe four times, paying a small fee to the organisers each time, to cover the cost of the awards. Gold dipper times will be in the region of five and a half minutes, second-class bronze will be gained in under eight minutes. Separate classes have become necessary for slalom K1, white-water racing craft, Canadian solos and even doubles. The times are adjusted by standards related to water levels. I did it in October 1961, and went right through the stopper after the 'Cauldron', a great rock and hole with stopper on the left at the top of the section called the 'Graveyard', because of the number of kayaks wrecked on each rock, and where every stone is a memorial.

Anyone may enter, and the events take place about six times during the year, when the anglers kindly allow the river to be used by canoeists.

Projecting ideas ahead, it is quite possible that really able white-water paddlers will be forced to seek the violence of sea tide races just offshore. Angling societies have battles with each other for water to fish on, so canoeists don't stand a great deal of chance of getting on to the really delectable rough river sections where anglers are to be seen enticing great fish to their hooks, having paid anything upwards of £50 for a day's fishing on some top-class rivers. One day's fishing would equip the ordinary canoeist for two or three years!

The difficulty with tide races is that they tend to tail off out to sea, and may run very powerfully for seven or eight miles, typically around headlands. If one should come unstuck on the Ramsay Island tide race off St David's Head, South Wales, then the chances of expiring helplessly in the Bristol Channel somewhere off Skokholm are very good. Such racing would put an impossible safety requirement on the organisers.

CANOE SLALOM
This branch of the sport is very popular with competitors and with spectators; recent commercial sponsorship has made an International event at Llangollen possible, and this has been seen in each of the last two years on TV. Judging by the comments heard after this, the public enjoys watching this colourful and exciting sport.

Canoeing is an Olympic sport now, and sprinters have been sprinting for many years in K1, K2, and K4, and at the time

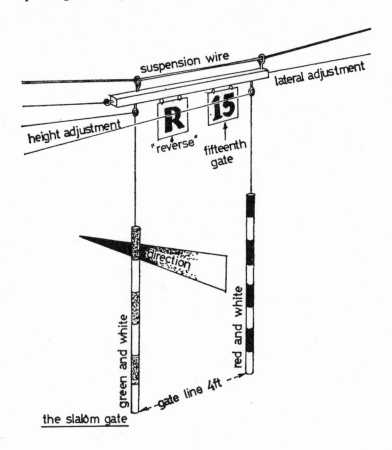

the slalom gate

of writing it was planned to include canoe slalom, for the first time, in 1972 in the Olympics at Augsburg in Germany. The British teams have been in the top five, and individual performers do well. In 1960 we had a gold medal in the world championships and in 1967 a silver medal. Maybe the first Olympic slalom event will find Britons among the medals. Undoubtedly this will stimulate interest and support for this branch of the sport in Britain. There are hopes that an artificial course will be built at Holme Pierrepoint near Nottingham, on a twelve-foot weir beside the Trent. The water flow there is 1,000 cubic feet per second on average, which is quite enough to supply all the water needed for top competition, at International level.

In canoe slalom a rough river is selected, about half a mile of it being suitable for a course. Not more than thirty gates are erected, and these can be anything from four feet to eleven feet in width, depending on their purpose. Some gates are taken downstream, some upstream, some forwards and some backwards. You can guarantee that the course planner will have introduced several nasty traps for the inexperienced to fall into.

The gates are numbered and must be taken in order, or penalties will be awarded. The gate poles are painted either red and white or green and white, denoting left hand and right hand poles respectively. Wrong presentation, such as going backwards through a forward gate, or forward through a forward gate but upside down, will all earn heavy time penalties. It is possible to get away with the canoe ends slipping under a high hanging gate, but if the river should rise, later paddlers will find that their clearances are altered.

The paddlers set off in order of the numbers which they wear. In local events we hold for schoolchildren in Oxford, numbers up to eighty are found. After that we run out of numbers. National ranking events will have numbers up to 300. Each paddler must have two runs, the better one to count. Some paddlers will enter several events, such as the team event, and the judges event (if they are helping with the judging) and the open event plus whatever division of the slalom world they are paddling in. On top of this are the team events, in which teams of three paddlers will attempt to go down the course as quickly as possible without faults, and on one gate the whole team must pass through within fifteen seconds, or penalties are awarded.

During the quite exhausting manoeuvres required the paddler may well capsize, and if he does and leaves his boat he has retired from that run; he may not empty out his boat and re-enter and carry on. If however, he rolls up and carries on, that is acceptable, except that a roll takes from two to ten seconds, depending on difficulty, and this is a time penalty, apart from the possibility of missing a gate.

References have been made to penalties being awarded. The paddler sets a certain time for the course, from the moment his bows break the gate line on the first gate, until his stern leaves the gate line on the last gate, or more usually, when he passes under the finish line stretched over the river. His time is measured in seconds, and to this time are added penalties, usually ten seconds, twenty seconds, or fifty seconds, depending on the nature of the infringement.

These penalties are awarded at each gate, if a paddler strikes a pole from the inside of the gate, with either boat, body, or paddle he scores ten points. If he strikes both poles, he scores twenty. If he goes the wrong way through, or misses the gate, he scores fifty. If a team fails to go through the team gate in fifteen seconds, that is fifty added to the total team score. Judging these infringements is very difficult, and much argument develops. At each slalom there is a judges' tent where differences are decided, and appeals dealt with.

Because of the shortage of judges it is necessary to ask paddlers to judge when not competing, and so club and personal loyalties and dislikes, even hatreds, are sometimes revealed in judges decisions. One judge at a national event is said to have fixed one man of a team running the lower end of the course with a fierce look, before he got to the gate, and screamed '*Fifty!*' at him at the top of his voice. The poor paddler fell over in surprise! This tale may be apocryphal, but another man in that team vouches for it. It became, in fact, a fifty penalty, because in his surprise the paddler missed the gate altogether.

One paddler in a third division event took part in place of his friend. He who entered was a Division Three paddler, not very able, but seeking promotion. The man who actually paddled, was a Division One paddler, at the top of the tree. When paddlers are all covered up with lifejackets, helmets and so on, probably long hair and whiskers as well, it becomes difficult to see who is which. However, one of the judges, a keen-eyed youth, spotted the difference in paddling style, and knowing both of them blew the story to the control tent, and the game was up.

The divisions, at present, are Novice, Three, Two, and One. All beginners start in the Novice division and gain promotion by going well at subsequent slaloms. It is possible to move from Novice to Division One in three months, but this is exceptional. Most people would progress from Novice to Division Three or possibly Two in one year, and then find themselves in Division One in the next year as a result of scoring percentages of the top man's time during the year, these percentages putting them high enough if they are good enough. The higher the division the more difficult the course.

Frankly, and you may have guessed it already, canoeing sport can be a game of crafty moves, dirty tricks, and in some types of races outright violence is used. If you enjoy this sort of thing, that's your scene, then enjoy it. Personally I always have the greatest doubts when young lads showing signs of progress want to go in for competition; do I encourage them or dissuade them? The National Director of Coaching in the magazine *Canoeing in Britain,* the official organ of the British Canoe Union, wrote in the December 1971 issue of two letters published earlier, which, he said, had reinforced the horror and repugnance towards competition which had been growing in him over the last few years.

Frankly, I forecast a time not far distant when thugs and bandits flourish in canoeing sport, and events will be decided by force majeur, and not on canoeing skill. Nature, one trusts will establish a balance before that unhappy day.

I must at this point put in the criticism of Dave Holmes, who read the manuscript of this book. It is too good to miss.

'It happens, I know, and therefore it is right and proper that you should mention it. But it would seem that you are biased. I'm a novice slalomist who competes at novice slaloms. At   in two weeks time I am entered in the C2 event.

I can't paddle C2 to save my life. I'm sure we will fall out but what the Hell, that's what slalom is all about. It will be *fun.* Go to any third div or novice event and you will find the vast majority of people there are only in it for the *fun*. Winning or losing is not important to them.

Talk about Division One slalom, thats different, but don't confuse it with hundreds of people who paddle for *fun*.'

RECORD BREAKING, AND DIFFICULT AND DANGEROUS VOYAGES

Competitive canoeing against natural forces and done solo can be likened to competitive rock climbing or mountaineering, a bit of a nonsense. However, like Everest, it will be done because it is there.

The Atlantic has been crossed by canoe on three occasions, sailing each time. These canoes were very stable, of the large Klepper Aerius type, with inflated air bag gunwales. Others have set out and not been seen again. One man was seen waving to an aircraft about fifty miles west of Ireland some years ago, but who he was and what happened to him is not known.

The Irish Sea has been crossed, and various trips made which are quite dangerous and demanding. One Scot and his wife went from the mainland of Scotland to St Kilda, and that is a long trip. He only had to be half a mile off course in the thick mist, and the next stop was America. They in fact rested in the shelter of a nearby small island and were able to cross to St Kilda the next morning, to be helped ashore by astounded soldiers with a landing craft. They stayed the week and came back on the landing craft. I'm pleased it worked out.

The Minch between mainland Scotland and the Outer Hebrides was crossed in ten hours in 1971 by a small group of Scots paddlers, including two schoolboys. That piece of water is inclined to be rough, but it was reasonably smooth when they went across. The trip from the Mull of Galloway to Point of Ayre, Isle of Man, has been made once or twice, as has the trip out from St Bees Head to the Isle of Man.

It is probably only a matter of time before people cross the North Sea from Norfolk to Holland, or from Scotland to Norway. A voyage by a Wayfarer dinghy from Scotland via the Faeroes to Norway was made some years ago, and they turned right over twice and were dismasted, and still managed to take film of the incredible journey.

In the same area, just before the turn of the century when Victoria was our Queen, two Eskimo fishermen from East Greenland were blown out to sea in their kayaks by a sudden storm. For thirty days, approximately, they supported each other, and when one died the other continued alone. A drifter off Aberdeen picked him up fifty miles out in the North Sea. He was brought ashore and the University made a great fuss of him. He recovered his health and strength, and went around as a guest of learned societies. Arrangements to return him to his home were being made when he caught influenza and died.

In 1971 a man kayaked around Britain solo in a kayak he made himself. He was wrecked in the Solway Firth and swam ashore. He experienced many difficulties and completed an epic voyage at a rate of about thirty miles a day.

In the eighteen-sixties, J. MacGregor, a Scottish solicitor, made many voyages in the canoe he called 'Rob Roy'. He made a great deal of money out of his lecture tours which followed, and gave most of it away. This was the time when the Prince of Wales was patron of the Royal Canoe Club on the Thames at Richmond. The Rob Roy was seen all over Germany, in the Alps, and in France and in Egypt on the Nile.

The Channel has of course been crossed on many occasions. Men, women, boys and girls cross it, usually in well-ordered and escorted groups. This exercise has to some extent lost its glamour, especially when it was crossed by Captain Crook and the late Ron Rhodes in a K2 in three hours and twenty minutes on Wednesday September 20th, 1961. Now some bright, sea-salty instructor from the Solent has ideas to cross from the Isle of Wight to Cherbourg. He reckons the sea should not be too difficult, but it is the traffic that bothers him. When tankers can collide with each other, what chance has a tiny dot on the water when the masts and superstructure of some oncoming mammoth vessel remain in the same straight line whatever one does?

To the best of my knowledge I hold the record for the

journey Wolsingham to Wearmouth, in December 1961, in eleven and a half hours. This was done on two successive days, and was quite slow. The distance is fifty-three miles, and is downhill all the way. However, I see that the students of Bede College in Durham were claiming the first ever-race on the Wear in 1970, and it could be that I am as wrong as they are. William Bliss made many voyages by canoe on British rivers in this century, and his book is a classic on the subject. Stanford's map of the canoeing rivers of Britain shows Bliss's highest point on the Wear at Wolsingham, way back in the twenties, and in the eighteen-sixties there were two active canoeing clubs on the Wear one at Sunderland. Records? There is nothing new under this sun.

Possibly the best known long-distance canoeing race is the Devizes-Westminster, about 120 miles, and the record stands at under twenty hours. It takes place each Easter, usually in freezing conditions, and strong men have broken down and wept, and others gone to hospital for months to cure their frostbitten faces and hands. It's not my idea of sport, but many people have done the race not once but many times and love it. The race is for doubles, kayaks or Canadians, and began by a wager among several touring types in the fifties. They didn't foresee the dedication to training necessary for the top teams to win. Incidentally, as before, dirty tricks are found. There have been accusations of running two teams to one boat, and in the dark it would be a clever marshal to spot the swap. At some handy portage the waiting pair take over and the first pair take a rest. It's impossible for honest paddlers to win against that kind of combination. I wish such 'winners' joy with their success.

Other records or difficult voyages will be found. In 1971 the Colorado River was run by an expedition from Britain, and was generously documented with many photographs and written reports. Mike Clarke, the Editor of the magazine *Canoeing,* went with them and can give much detail of the trip. Vol 11, No. 10, published in December 1971, is devoted to the report of the voyage in the tracks of Powell, the American geographer, over a hundred years before. Each year the Canoe Camping Club takes a group to Finland and penetrates really remote lands by fast river, within the Arctic Circle. And there are usually men in their sixties in that group.

What do I think about canoe competition? Not much as it now is, but don't take my word for it, talk to a rabid enthusiast complete with scars, and ask him. He probably finds the catharsis of a personal confrontation necessary for his mental health.

Canoeing surfing galas are spreading in popularity in Britain. The latest I have heard about is well north of Edinburgh. The Surf Lifesaving Association of Great Britain has its own regional and national surfing galas. The emphasis is more upon reel and line drills, and so on, but the craft used, the surf skis, are becoming more and more like kayaks except for the deck and cockpit system used.

Time having passed since this book was first written, the pious hope expressed on p.146 has been revealed for what it is. However, Doug Parnham did come 7th overall, a very good result in the K1 events at Montreal. There was not a white water or slalom event at Montreal.

CHAPTER FOURTEEN

Some Good Canoeing Spots

There is enjoyment in solitude, and Britain's hundreds, thousands of miles of coastline offer a great deal to me that I haven't seen yet and maybe never shall. In some way this book is counter-productive. Out of my enjoyment of the sport, the book finds print; and if it succeeds, then the remote places come a little nearer, the lonely places lose their solitude. Don't worry, though. I'll be finding places I haven't even dreamed of yet; and there's enough for everyone.

The following examples are few in number, but archetypal of the kind of canoeing I have enjoyed, and still enjoy, and hope to continue to enjoy. Much of it is lonely and remote, but much is among heavily populated places, and these two conditions are not incompatible.

THE THAMES
Oxford. Launch at Donnington Bridge, beside Riverside Centre. You must have a Thames Conservancy Licence for your canoe. You get these from nearest lock-keeper, in this case Iffley Lock, half a mile downstream. There is plenty of parking space at Riverside.
Choice trips are as follows:
1. Parson's Pleasure, 6 miles return. Go upstream from Donnington Bridge, turn right up Cherwell river in half mile, take left fork half a mile, take right fork just under Magdalen Bridge, carry on up the Cherwell, to weir which is beside the nude bathing place at Parson's Pleasure. A notice here

requests ladies please to leave their boats here and rejoin them upstream. Male partners in boats may then take the boat through the bathing place behind decorous sight screens. It is noteworthy that the University canoe club LD race goes right through this lot, but as it is usually early in the spring there is no one swimming there. There are little streams to the West of the Cherwell, but to venture on to these is to find yourself on private waters.

2. Folly Bridge and back, 2½ miles. Go upstream from Donnington straight up the Thames, noticing the University

Boat Houses. Go up under the stone bridge called Folly
Bridge, keeping right. On the right by the Steamer Depot
is a tiny stinking ditch which goes up into Christchurch
meadows. Here it enters a drain, which you enter at your
peril. In calm weather with no surface water draining off it is
possible to go about 2,000 feet underground and to explore
the drains under Carfax, and T. E. Lawrence (of Arabia),
when at Oxford, is reputed to have done this in a canoe.
Upstream, under the bridge, one can go to the far left-hand
of the river and enter a pool on the upstream side of the
bridge beside some boat-yard sheds. Here there are three
arches leading under the Abingdon Road. The Thames flows
through them. The southernmost arch leads into a private
pool in a garden with a way out under the house. There are
guard railings down across the archway but these have been
bent and canoeists can squeeze through. The middle arch
under the road leads through a jungly thicket beside a workshop tip, and the first or northernmost arch leads into a
covered boat-yard pool where cruisers lie under cover. Return
to the Donnington Bridge, and on the way explore little side
turns, notably one on the right going downstream, beside the
University Boat House, and one on the left which runs
through lovely woodland behind the College boat houses and
joins the Cherwell about quarter of a mile from its confluence
with the Thames.

3. From Wolvercote to Donnington Bridge, 6 miles. Take
two cars, and carry the canoes to the car park beside the
swimming pool at Wolvercote, to the north of Oxford. Then
do a shuttle to Donnington Bridge, leaving the other car
there. Launch beside the bridge beside the car park beside
the swimming station at Wolvercote. Paddle downstream,
and in about quarter of a mile there is the weir for Godstow
Lock on the right. If the weir is running there is a fairly
powerful return flow to one side, and only people with
slalom-type craft and suitable· experience should play with
it, otherwise you will be sucked in sideways, rolled over and
the canoe devoured; survival could be a problem too.

Another half mile and the Perch Inn on the right bank is
well worth a visit early on a hot summer's afternoon (pre-

ferably out of term, otherwise there is a queue of people waiting to be served). A short way further one comes to Medley Boat Station. The Thames goes straight on, under an old iron bridge, and to the left is a boat yard and a large notice that states 'Danger. Not Navigable'. Well, I have on several occasions gone exploring there and, through a wilderness of reeds and pleasant pools and swans and anglers, have found a way for a canoe.

The stream meanders by meadow and bush and reed until it arrives beside a car parking place where there is a low bridge, under which one can go. Force a way through the reeds and then under a very low railway bridge. Again passage is possible if you tuck your head in. Then follows about a mile of paddling along a stream alongside the canal, and at a lower level. Where the lock gate to the canal is found, the canal goes off to the right to rejoin the Thames, but our stream goes straight on and into the western side of the centre of Oxford. Beside a decorative garden and under two low bridges goes the very pleasant river, but beware after the second bridge. If the water is flowing fast, and the weir gates by the castle wall are open, there is a danger of being pulled through them and possibly trapped. However, a portage up a vertical stone wall on the right is possible if taken in good time. If the weir is closed, as it normally is during low flow rates in summer, then it is possible to go right up to the gate and portage right beside it. One chap lost his glasses here, immediately plunged in neck deep beside the weir gate, then reached down and picked up his spectacles first try. The portage is not easy, and the drop on the far side is quite considerable, but the water is only about a foot deep there. Most people lower their canoes to the water then scramble down the masonry, and then climb in from knee-deep water.

From here the river continues down through Oxpens, the open market area, by new college buildings, and a contributory stream on the right going down leads back up under the Post Office, up a gentle rapid under the building, and then under the walls of a brewery, where you should look out for squirts of hot water from pipes high on the wall. At the top end of this stretch is a weir gate and a derelict water wheel that has beautiful old iron parts. I'd very much like to see it working again.

About half a mile downstream the confluence with the Thames occurs just under the railway bridge. To the right anarchist writings appear on the walls. One I especially enjoy is 'No man is fit to be a leader' ... Yet here is the writer attempting to lead opinion. Another half mile brings one to the Folly Bridge, and from there it is a mile to Donnington Bridge.

To conclude on Oxford, there are many miles of interesting backwaters and places to be seen from these waterways. There are some awkward places requiring real skill to negotiate, and some which bring out the schoolboy satisfactions of scrambling about on places where people would not normally go, but canoeing lends a reason for trying it.

RIVER WEAR

Tod Hills to Durham. This is a grade two river in normal conditions, although once in a flash flood it was in high spate and mostly grade three with touches of grade four. There is a bridge on a side road at Willington where it crosses to the hamlet of Tod Hills. Beside the bridge is a field to which access is usually free although it is private, and local people go there on hot summer days; it is a good swimming place. Launch the canoes here, and then go downstream to Durham. Mostly the river is a series of stony shallows, with long calm pools between.

In two miles is Page Bank, which was once a busy mining community and is now derelict. In another two miles one comes to a high railway viaduct and soon after this there is a weir under the old bridge at Croxdale. The Bridge Inn, as it was, has in the past tolerated wet canoeists very well, and this is one of the high-class hotels in Durham. Another mile and a half to Butterby Scar, and here the river meanders about over great flat slabs of rock. One can find a way down it, but it is usually very shallow and bump and scrape. Then the river wanders about and after Shincliffe bridge it goes on to Durham.

Some Good Canoeing Spots

During the season, many people bring hired rowing boats up this far, and racing oarsmen from the school, city and University crews must be afforded right of way. Well, if you were busily engaged on hurtling through life backwards, you'd want to be sure things were getting out of your way, wouldn't you? Under the first bridge at Durham, there is a half mile or so of beautiful wooded scenery beside the cathedral and castle, and then there is the first weir. This can easily be shot far left as you approach it from upstream. This was the first place I ever experienced white water. Shoot through here, and go on towards the second bridge and the second weir. You can pull out on the left just above the weir, or even in low water climb out on top of the dry exposed weir top. Here a way down can be seen on the left, in three steps. Each step has a narrow slot in it, about two feet wide, and if you don't get it right thats too bad. Make up your mind if you are skilful enough to shoot it, and if you are, whether you *will* shoot it. If the answer is no on both or either count, then you can portage from the bank side about a hundred yards above the weir on the left-hand side, and there is a car park there which provides a handy pick-up point. If you do shoot it, make sure that your footrest is firm, because if you miss the slots you will find the canoe will stop whilst you career on through your footrest. Which could be nasty.

That whole trip is about eleven miles, but if you want to go on from here a quite exciting piece of river follows down to Finchale (pronounced 'Finkle') Abbey. This is another five miles of interesting river; there is a café at Finchale Abbey, and the ruins of the Abbey itself are well worth a visit. This road is found via Framwellgate Moor and Brasside. Stopping at the Abbey can be fraught with episodes; there was one mighty paddler we all knew, Jim Meston, who shot through here so fast he didn't notice the crowd and the pull-out and he went as far as Chester Le Street before he realised that he had come too far, and that was another four miles. If you don't make the breakout before the footbridge, you have a long haul back, because a low and heavily wooded cliff prevents access further along.

THE SEA

The first place ever I went on the sea in a canoe was at a place called Ganavan Sands near Oban, but I was ten then, and it wasn't serious. However, when I began sea canoeing in earnest, it was at Hartlepool, in Durham. You can tackle this if you can handle a canoe with some idea of responsibility. *Hartlepool.* Go to the 'Battery' where the guns were placed that fired on the German cruisers that bombarded Hartlepool in the First World War. My father was on that battery at that time, and if was an odd feeling for me to wander around the old battery buildings where the Hartlepool Kayak Club used to be, and maybe still is, and think of that. The Coast-guard sits in a tower beside the lighthouse, so seek him out and explain your business and get his advice, on the sea and wind and weather.

Carry the canoes down to the promenade which is built over an old burial ground from the monastery,* and you will go down some steps to the end of the breakwater. Launching is possible from a sandy beach in the shelter of the breakwater.

If you are not skilful on the sea, go along towards the harbour on your right as you launch from the beach, and potter about among the jetties and wharves. Go right across to the other side, where a ferry used to run before Middleton Bridge was built. Go around the jetty end on that side, and you will find a way into Middleton Harbour, which is difficult to enter if there is a swell running, as there often is. The wave patterns rebound and swill about in the harbour entrance, and it can be quite exciting if you can handle your canoe. If you can't then it could be shipwreck, and a wet scramble up the steps on the Northern arm of the harbour wall. The water is typical North Sea, cold, grey and humping about on the horizon most horribly.

There is surfing to be had at Seaton Sands, about three miles south, and an expedition to Seal Sands in the Tees Estuary is a good four-hour voyage, but look out for sea-

*This low cliff crumbled in a storm in 1922, when my parents had a house and a garden there, and opened up several old graves complete with skeletons.

going ships charging out between the North Gare and the South Gare at Teesmouth.

One can paddle north to Seaham and then Sunderland and South Shields, but that is a long way. Just north of Sunderland is Whitburn Ranges, and the best thing to do is to come very close inshore there, and go tight under the shelter of the low cliffs. This is where coal is washed up on to the beach and the stumps of an ancient petrified forest can be seen about half a mile out to sea, at very low spring tides.

Swanage. You can take your canoes to the promenade road at Swanage, offload, then park the cars back in car parks away from the beach. Launch from the beach, then go east towards Old Harry Rocks. A tide race runs along the mile or so of cliff face here, and the cliff is mostly chalk, which is like grease if one is stepping on to a ledge by the water. Right at the end of Old Harry, a vertical column of chalk, are Old Harry's Wife, and Parson's Barn, other nearby columns. At the end of this line of cliff face is a series of ways through caves and cuttings to Studland Bay and further on, Poole Harbour. It can be quite rough in the tide race off Old Harry, but two minutes through the rock or round the headland, and all is calm and smooth. We went around Old Harry, and some of the group were quite clearly not able to paddle back to Swanage beach. They landed at Studland Beach, whilst the rest of us returned for the cars at Swanage.

Unknown to us at that time, Studland Beach is privately owned, and you will be asked about 35 new pence for landing there, and the people also claim an unusual right in that they own the land down to low water mark, not high water mark as is usual almost everywhere in Britain. We had a rather nasty passage of arms here, and had it not been that some of the group were too shattered to go on, we would have left by sea. I for one will never again trouble these people with my pennies or presence; and it's not really sour grapes, for that bay is calm, flat and from my point of view rather uninteresting. But Swanage Bay is another matter altogether.

West from Swanage Bay one finds tide races around headlands, such as Peveril Point, Anvil Head, St Aldhems Head, Swyre Head and Kimmeridge Ledges. There is also a little opening in the cliffs, which is noted on a locally drawn map in a lovely pub in Kingston, nearby, as being dignified with the name 'Scratch Arse Hole'. I can only ponder on the stark realism of the fishermen who doubtless named it.

Further west one comes to the army ranges beyond Kimmeridge Bay where tanks fire shells at things. I don't want to end being tracked by a radar-directed computerised cannon, so I stay away from those ranges when the red flag is flying. Just here in Kimmeridge Bay one can see what is reputed to be the only producing oil well in Great Britain. There is also a good car park at Kimmeridge and easy access to the water, but Chapman's Pool is on private land, there is a charge to enter it, and the portage off the beach, which is undistinguished slate, mud and gravel, is best described as fiendish after a hard day paddling along the cliffs. This part of the Dorset Coast is for able canoeists.

Tre-Addurr Bay, Anglesey. Go to Anglesey, and four miles short of Holyhead, at Valley crossroads at the traffic lights, turn left towards Tre-Addurr Bay. A winding road leads there, and a camp site can be found at Raven's Head, just east of the bay, on the headland. Launch in the bay from beautiful sands, or from one of the tiny bays along the headland promontory. I haven't been east from here yet, but several times have gone west. Tide races really hurtle about on this exposed cliff coast, and the waves can be quite exciting. The strata in the cliff face are so twisted and knotted, that the nearest description I can give is that of knotted root wood from some gnarled hedgerow tree.

The cliff face is riddled with caves and the rush and slosh of the sea waves. Seal quite often pop up and look about, but there are many subaqua people there too, so don't mistake one for the other. One diver I was talking to told me that during the mating season in spring the randy male seals will cruise along underwater beside a diver and give him the odd playful nudge or nibble. The nudge can consist of a full-grown bull seal coming head on at a speed of about fifteen miles an hour to crash into one's neoprene clad belly; or the nibble is from above and behind as the inquisitive male explores from that region. Quite unnerving he said, especially when one is thirty feet deep. A full trip around South Stack and North Stack will depend on tide races and how able one is. Able novices could potter about Tre-Addurr Bay, whilst more able people in competent groups can go further round the coast. The social life in the holiday season is first-class, but the place gets crowded.

Farne Islands, Holy Island, Northumberland. Go north on the A1 road until you come to a place called Beal. It is simply a hamlet with a filling station and hotel, and an old school which is now an outdoor education centre for Northumberland Education Authority. Turn right and go to Holy Island, noting that it is no use trying this during the period from two hours before high tide to three hours after, as the causeway is flooded by the sea. Drive over on to the island, and then go carefully along the sand flats on the island side for two miles until the road turns off into the village. The tiny port of Holy Island is well worth a stroll around, and Lindisfarne is an old ruin with a great history.

Take the canoes to the harbour side, and launch there. Do not launch at spring tides or in strong offshore winds, because the next stop is Holland, and you will probably be unprepared for a voyage of that length (although it is not beyond the bounds of possibility that a small expert group could cross the North Sea in about four days by kayak, with a following breeze). If the tide is coming in, paddle around the harbour, then go off up the Gut and around the back of the island. If you time it right your transport can be back on the mainland waiting to pick you up by the causeway, but you must be sure that you arrive there just about two hours before the full tide or else there is a long tedious portage across mud to where the road is. Much easier to float up to your transport.

On the open side of the island is the Plough-stick, and seal abound in this area. Here it was I saw a canoeist watching a seal. He was being tailed by another seal, and watching all this was another canoeist, and watching him was another seal, and they were all in a long line, Indian file. I was of course watching all this, but what was watching me? I'll never know. On the north end of the island is a surfing beach, I am told, but I've not been there yet. To the south, about four or five miles, is the group called the Farne Islands.

If you are camping at Waren Mill (and it is a good camp site, but book up in advance for the summer months), then you could launch at high tide into Budle Bay. At low tide this is a waste of mud and sand and tussocks of sea grass, and it is not very good. Better to go to the cliff top car park just south of Bamburgh Castle, about a mile. The Coastguard lookout is there and the launching place is called Greenhill Rocks. There is beautiful sand here and long beaches with plenty of room for surfing without interfering with swimmers. The board riders are mostly down in Cornwall. Go up and talk with the coastguard and let him know if you intend to cross to Farne. He will let you know of the forecasts and perhaps show you round his lookout and tell you of some of the incidents involving coastal craft.

Cross to Inner Farne, that is about a mile and a quarter, and we usually go north of the island if the tide is flooding, or south if it is ebbing. On the north end is the Churn, which can spout froth and foam up to thirty feet high, provided that the set of the waves is from the north-east. If you land on Inner Farne, have about 35 pence handy because a man with a cash bag will request payment if you wish to land at Cuthberts Landing. However, a visit is worth it. We stood in knee-deep water and emptied out a canoe before carrying on, so we avoided payment as we didn't really go ashore. All around here are nesting birds, which are protected by the National Trust and other authorities.

Further across Cuthberts Sound is the long ridge of the Cuthberts Bridge, and the Wideopens and the Knocklin reef and the Kettle. Seal live here and are often to be seen. This sound is only about six feet deep and the tide swills through like a grade two river rapid. Beyond the bridge is Staple Sound, and that is about one and a half miles across. On the far side is Gun Rock. A fairly hefty tide race concentrates just off the rock, and waves can pile up and double here with crests rising to ten to twelve feet in an otherwise almost calm sea. Of course this is only with the tide running, one can plan the crossing to occur at neap tides between half tide flows, i.e., at an hour before the turn, or up to an hour after. The fastest run of the tide is at half tide, about three hours after the turn.

Beyond Gun Rock is Staple Island and Brownsman, and these have resident populations of rare birds and students looking after them. There are large notices stating 'No Landing'. What we would do if someone had to go ashore urgently I don't know. South of this lot is the Bluecaps and the Pinnacles. Waterways run behind these rocks and the wave and tide surges through and this gives some really frightening white water for experts to play with.

We were told that a killer whale had been making tasty snacks of seal for the last week, and so we were on the look out for the tell-tale fin slicing through the water. It is said that a killer whale could take a canoe in its jaws and nip it in half in a flash. I did feel a little naked at this place. Further out to the south is the Callers, a reef (pronounced with a short 'a' as in 'hat') and the Fang Rock and Crumstone. Lovely, weird, eerie names. Man, you should see the sea piling over the Callers, a nasty devouring curl fifteen feet high and roaring alone six miles out from the coast.

Further east is the Longstone Rock, and the lighthouse where Grace Darling lived and fame made her name immortal. The flat reef of the Harcars on which the *Forfarshire* was wrecked is a roost for seal colonies. These seal families must have nurseries for the pups, else why did we see three or four adult females on a lonely rock (Roddam and Green) with something like a hundred pups all around cavorting about in the water and on the rock? Conservationist people have defended the seal population of these reefs and islets very vigorously against the attacks of fishermen, who say that the seal kill salmon and damage the nets. The defence of the seal has been that they are such docile creatures and not fierce.

However, under the watchful eyes of the conservationists,

the seal population has grown and grown and now territorial demands are becoming so fierce, that outbreaks of killing and anti-social behaviour by the seals themselves has been noticed. Now the conservationists must agree to selective culling (an in-word for 'killing') of the seal population.

Landing on Outer Farne, or Longstone is possible beside a notice which says 'No Landing' Do not be put off by that, it refers to a fenced off area to the south end of the rocks. Arctic Tern will attack anyway, so stay low in the cleft in the rocks where you land, and don't break the skyline. A stroll on the rock invites attack by a swarm of these small white and black birds which wheel around one's head like flies on a hot summer day by the river. The noise they kick up is out of all proportion to their size, and can be frightening. Daphne DuMaurier's story 'The Birds' comes to mind. The return trip takes about two hours and can be quite exciting. Cold is the main pain I find after a day out there.

CHAPTER FIFTEEN

Some Canoeing Yarns

Canoeing has many stories attached to it. Some of these are based on mythology, and some based on events which happened. Some of those I will describe happened to me, and some to others.

THE CROSSING OF THE IRISH SEA

This is one of the great one day voyages which is possible for skilled and fit sea canoeists. The voyage was described in the April 1970 issue of the magazine *Canoeing*. Those who went on it were Nick Gough, Derek Mayes, and Dave Bland, all people involved in instructing canoeing at Outdoor Activity Centres in North Wales. They had intended to travel towards Ireland in their kayaks, but the prevailing wind which was expected to shift did not, and so they had to make the run from Ireland towards Wales.

They set out on the Holyhead – Dun Laoghaire ferry on June 28th, 1969, and when they arrived at Dun Laoghaire the harbour authorities were unfavourably impressed by the idea. However, having delivered a homily on the futility of setting out on such a voyage, they left them to it, and at 01.00 on 29th the group of three set out and steered by the Kish Bank Light. They paddled in the dark for three hours, but the night was fairly bright and they could see each other and their surroundings quite easily.

Came the dawn, and they were out of sight of land in a thin mist, which limited their range of vision. They took magnetic bearings on various high-lying clouds, and steered by them for ten minutes at a time, then again checked direction by compass. As they were very much along the ferry track, they found that bags of rubbish thrown overboard attracted seagulls which wheeled about the floating debris, in the form of a cone of birds with the apex downwards and pointing at the rubbish. These cones of birds were quite noticeable throughout the day, and made a useful check on direction.

Later in the day, when they had been out of sight of land for some hours, and confidence was ebbing a little, they noticed high-lying cloud, of the typical standing wave variety, and were of the opinion that the great bulk of Snowdon was forcing the airflow upwards and thus causing this cloud. They were correct, after steering towards that cloud they soon saw land, and recognised the high cliffs of Holy Mountain by Holyhead. This is typical of one form of navigation used by Pacific Islanders in their staggering 5,000 mile canoe journeys. And the Maori word for New Zealand, incidentally, means "land of the long White Cloud'.

In the late afternoon they were in full sight of Holyhead harbour, but between them and it was the fast-running tide race that whirls by North Stack and out around the Skerries where King Charles' ship is sunk. They had to cross this three miles of tide race, and not pile up on the rocks or in the overfalls, and in their state they were not really ready for flat-out, white-water canoeing, although they had been in conditions at least as bad before.

Then came a two-hour battle to cover three miles to the entrance to Holyhead harbour, by the end of the long breakwater. They made it, but Nick was in a state of collapse, and seemed asleep in his canoe. They beached on a shingle bank just inside the harbour and Nick revived, he'd just wanted a little kip before going on. They landed before dark at the harbour, and collected their car. They all agreed that the drive back to the Centre in the mountains was the worst part of the journey, as weariness was heavy upon them.

They had had all kinds of technical help on the crossing, and had selected with great care what they were to eat, and they rank among the top men in deep-water canoeing. This crossing does not equate with the North Face of the Eiger for danger and difficulty, but it is one of the most difficult sea trips that canoeists have done in recent years. The three men had built up experience on other unusual and difficult sea trips before trying this one.

Other canoeists have crossed from the tip of south-west Scotland to the Isle of Man, which is quite a difficult trip. Another long one that some people have their eye on is from Land's End to Wolf Rock light and then to the Scillies, which is reasonably possible in a day. I'm told that the tide races and rock formations around the Scillies are really fascinating from the cockpit of a kayak.

Most astonishing of all is to discover that the Atlantic has been crossed from East to West on three occasions; by kayak by Captain Romer (Germany, 1928), and twice by a Dr Lindbergh.

RAMSAY SOUND AND THE NORTH BISHOP
In August 1968 Les Guest and I arrived at Whitesand Bay by St David's Head in South Wales, looking for surf, but found eighteen-inch ripples, About midday we set out to paddle in two slalom kayaks to the North Bishop rock which lay due west, about four miles out. The air was hardly moving, the waves were flat, the sun shone and it was pleasantly warm and calm.

Soon we passed the end of St David's Head and the coast-line to the north opened out craggy and high. The sea had developed a curious hump-and-hollow shape that moved around uncertainly, but it was quite small and easy to handle. After about ten minutes of steady paddling, we found to our surprise that St David's Head had receded at a tremendous rate, not eastwards behind us, but northwards. The only con-clusion was that we were heading south at a fair rate. Still, North Bishop was near, and we were down-tide of a reef of flat rocks (called Carreg Trai on the chart).

Here we made more progress towards the North Bishop and found a swirling but slow-moving whirlpool by the side of it. Entering on the east side of this pool we stopped paddling, and the great wheeling patch of water carried us around like a roundabout or carousel, and we slipped easily into a cleft in the rocks. Grey seal were lying on the rocks and watched us with a little interest. Looking back towards the mainland, I had a very nasty shock. The area we had just crossed in the last hour was now a turbulent mass of standing waves. The tide race caused by the vast movement of the Irish Sea Southward through St George's Channel gained speed. It was horrible, and the rumble of its power reached us a mile off.

It was at this point that I realised what was happening. We had launched at high tide, before the tide race started, and so we had been well across as it was starting to pick up speed, and now it was roaring through the Sound, going faster as it reached its half-tide peak rate of movement. Tension made me feel ill. Behind was a welter of impossible water. Ahead, through the narrow gap in the rocks, lay the open Atlantic, and maybe some peace, some chance to escape this mad, racing water. We eased our way gently into the cleft, and I went first. On the other side I met a humping, cresting wave that lofted over me and threatened to drop on me. As we sailed up towards it crest, I spun the slalom boat around like a top, and the surging crest dropped me across Les's rear deck, as he had turned. We surfed through the gap in the rocks, my canoe sliding about and banging on the other canoe.

No way that way. However, as we circled on the great wheeling patch of water it was seen that the water towards Carreg Rhoson was smooth and not breaking, although the waves were standing high. We curved across the mile and half of water quite easily, but worry was making me ill. Les grinned at my anxious questions. 'Anything you say, Alan. Its your expedition. I have the utmost confidence in your ability. Nothing to worry about here.' I wished very much that I had a fraction of his confidence, for terror was gripping me. Maybe I looked less upset than I felt.

We had a bite to eat and a sip of drink, and after taking a transit, that is a line-up of two noticeable marks on land (in this case, the cliffs at the north end of Ramsay Island, and a white farmhouse on the hill on the mainland beyond,)

we set off. Although the tide was sweeping southwards
through the two-mile-wide sound, we could ferry glide across
it by angling our bows to the north-east, the northerly component of our movement stemming the tide and the easterly
component giving us progress over the ground. This was fine
until we hit the main strength of the tide about half a mile
from Carreg Rhoson, and we soon found ourselves paddling
flat out due north, and slowly slipping south towards a
seething maelstrom of water roaring over the rocks of Llech
Uchaf, which looks a bit like a submarine conning tower
standing out of the water. Casting caution away, for there
was nothing left but a little time, we sprinted off pointing
due east, and trusting that we had enough zip to cross above
the overfalls before we were swept into them by the tide,
which must have been running about five, possibly six
knots.

We did clear the overfalls, but entered crossing standing
waves, just like a river rapid, only in this case the waves had
about 45 degrees face slope, and the whole of the canoe, fourteen feet long, was laid on the wave face. We were standing
on the footrests, with the bows nudging down into the wave
trough and nearly diving, and the stern up behind with the
curling wave crests just hung over it. We estimated that the
wave height was 10 feet. The spray tumbled down about my
head, and the sweat ran off me, and the salt in my eyes was
very painful. We edged our way across that gulf, and trod
warily.

We did reach a cleft in the western cliffs of Ramsay Island
just south of Aber Mawr. Here we were given a lift by a
passenger-carrying fishing boat, the Puffin (which plies for
hire from St David's), and eventually we were slipped over
the side after a fascinating ride round the south end of
Ramsay and up Ramsay Sound by the Bitches to Point St
John. Soon we arrived at the beach at Whitesand, five
minutes before our estimated time of arrival, five p.m. Our
friends were pleased to see such punctuality, but the story
fair puzzled them. Now I know Ramsay Sound fairly well,
having been there again in July 1971, but this time it was
fairly flat, and although fast-moving not particularly difficult.

So don't try that one unless you are in company with expert sea canoeists.

THE CASE OF THE EMBARRASSED COASTGUARD

In 1968 I was in charge of a group of sixteen young men from the youth service in Staffordshire. With me also were five adults. There were four quite experienced canoeists in the group to begin with, but by now, with a five-day trip down the Tweed from Drumelzier to Kelso behind us, we were all pretty fit. All the equipment was in good order except for one canoe which had a strained seam on the rear deck which was seeping water, but not too badly.

We called at the Coastguard Station and spoke to the same Coastguard on two separate occasions, and he was convinced that we knew what we were doing with flares, and self-rescue capacity, and a knowledge of the many rocks and islets that comprise the Farnes. I had been there three times before.

We left one morning in a gentle south-easterly breeze, force three Beaufort. When we arrived at Inner Farne, we were met by the keeper who wanted to charge us each a 3s. 6d. landing fee, but we only had a few pence among the lot of us. I negotiated a group charge and gave him my home address to send the bill to, but, as a point of interest, it did not arrive. By this time one of our members was already feeling ill, and another found that his boat was leaking badly. The slightly choppy waves and the exit through the surf line from Greenhill rocks had opened up the already strained seam, and it gaped for about a foot.

The groups split up, and I took nine, including four adults, out towards the Longstone Light by Staple Sound. The other six returned with an experienced instructor in charge and went round the island to have a good look at it. The 'Cauldron' on the north side of the island was blowing great fountains of spray into the sunny air, and it fell sparkling all around. It's a dangerous place, for if one fell into that there'd be no rescue, just a vertical ride thirty feet into the air to fall on hard granite.

We had an interesting journey by Gun Rock tide race in

Staple Sound, and by Brownsman, and Sunderland Hole to Longstone where we landed and were mobbed by Arctic terns. Eventually we returned to the mainland to find our separated group had been in difficulties. Between Inner Farne and the mainland, about a third of the way across the Fairway, Graham had found his boat to be too full to handle properly. He chatted with the leader and then tipped out to do a deep-water rescue, and so empty the canoe. This they did quite smartly, and on they went. As they neared the surf line, they saw an inshore rescue boat streaking up the surf line from Seahouses, and it stopped beside them 'You in trouble?' they were asked. 'No,' was the reply, but they made a serious mistake. Instead of letting the Instructor in charge do the talking, Graham came across to chat as well, about a hundred yards from the beach and in full view of the three Landrovers with hot soup and dry clothes. The rest surfed in with varying degrees of ability and this horrified the local fishermen, who were unused to this sort of 'wild' behaviour in boats.

Then, quietly, without fuss, Graham's boat sank under him. 'Excuse me,' said he, and made as to swim ashore, a not impossible task for a strong swimmer like him. However, with the light of challenge in their eyes, the rescue craft men hauled the waterlogged boat out of the sea, and so great was the weight of water within it, and so considerable their strength, that they broke its back as they hauled it out. Graham was hauled in just as quickly, and being shy and lacking boldness to leap out and swim for his soup and clothing, allowed himself to be 'rescued'. As he said, later it wasn't so much the very fast, very bumpy and wet ride back to Seahouses, nor the annoyance of the fishermen at being called out for a non-rescue, it was arriving soggy and wet on the harbour steps, to haul his busted boat on to the harbour side, and there to stand and wait for fifteen minutes until one of the Land-Rovers could catch up with him. And with only one plimsoll on, too.

As we arrived, (all this had happened two hours before,) Graham himself told me the story. I changed, and went to see the Coastguard and apologise, although for the life of me

I couldn't see why. Well, he apologised to me, so there we were apologising helpfully to each other. He had by chance, been watching the group return. He had relieved the man to whom I had spoken earlier. He had the note about self-rescue capacity and flares and E.T.A., etc., but it didn't make much sense. That is, if you've never seen a waterlogged canoe rescued by another canoe in two minutes, then you really find it hard to believe.

Through the telescope eyepiece, Graham was seen to capsize after obviously being in some difficulty for a little time. Immediately the Coastguard did all that was necessary to set a rescue under way. About three or four minutes later, after all the necessary phone calls had been made, the Coastguard was incredulous to find the group much nearer shore, and paddling happily along, no signs of distress, and the group as before. He counted them a dozen times, to make sure, and he could recognise the hefty chap in the leaking canoe, but still it was true, they were O.K. Meanwhile, trailing a rooster tail of spray, the rescue craft from Seahouses was belting up from the south, and not having radio it was impossible to recall it, except by flare.

We talked for a while, and I went and apologised to two rather fed-up looking fishermen next day. Mind, as they said, it's impossible to tell a well-organised canoeing group from a bunch of incompetents (not quite the word they used!), and when something like that happens then what does one do? Let them drown? That is a true Fingalism, as explained in the next story . . .

FINGAL

There is a great folk history in Celtic mythology concerning a giant who lived in Ireland and Scotland, and who flung rocks at other giants, hence the Isle of Man, one of his badly aimed missiles. He was called Fionn mac Cumhaill, or Finn McCool, or Fingal. All manner of incredible things happened when he was about, and a great leader and king was he.

Up on the Tyne just before the war was Oliver Cock, recently our National Canoeing Coach, or Director of Coaching as he now is. He was a draughtsman, and one of the draughtsman's tales to explain some of the inexplicable happenings in drawing offices, is to invoke Sod's Law, which roughly goes as follows:

If you drop a piece of jam and bread, it will fall jammy side down on the carpet, and thus be all hairy when picked up.

You may wish to discuss the Law with your companion who has not seen the unfortunate happening, and, explaining it to him, you drop a piece of jam and bread on to the carpet, by way of demonstration, and it falls jammy side *up*.

This is the elementary proof of Sod's Law!

Well now, that is a rough way of describing what every canoeist knows applies to him. He drives home from a week-end event and the setting sun is in his eyes and he can't see clearly whichever way he turns his car, or so it seems. He stops at a wayside pub to let the sun go down, and when he eventually gets out at closing time he can't even see the road.

I hasten to point out that most canoeists are the essence of sobriety, but they are subject to the attentions of Fingal from time to time, and he it is who is the custodian of cussedness and sees to it that Sod's Law is given effect.

A few years ago a Fingal club was formed, and it has a distinctive tie in a disgusting shade of yellow, with a little black representation of Fingal, a cheerful little chap. All proceeds go to help the funds of the Canoe Lifeguard Scheme.

Well, about that time I was in charge of the canoeing activities of a group of army officers at Hambledon Weir. We were using the Chalfont Park Clubhouse, which is on an island about thirty feet from the mainland where the cars were parked. John, the Adjutant, had to return with all speed to the camp where he was to attend some important social function. He changed on the island into his pukka gear, cavalry twill trousers, cravat, suede boots, the lot. The very essence of elegance he looked, standing waiting for me to ferry him across in an old and large Canadian canoe. We loaded up all the bags for the rest of the group, and they were kidding John that Fingal would get him. John replied that all would be well as Alan would take him safely across the water, and so it was.

John reached down from the five-foot, steep grass bank on the other side as I passed out all the bags to him, which he placed beside the car park. I paddled away a short distance and he turned to wave to his fellow men shouting ribald things from the island. 'You see?', said he 'Fingal . . . whoops!' – and his feet shot out from under him as he slid, to end standing knee-deep in muddy water, his beautiful clothing a shambles. The men on the island, of course, cried for pure happiness!

On p.169 I refer to various crossings of large pieces of ocean. Less than a week ago, as I write, I read in the magazine *Canoeing* that the trip from Sennen Cove to the Scillies by way of Wolf Rock lighthouse has been done. That is about 30 miles of sea. You may have read that Derek Hutchinson attempted to cross from Felixstowe to Belgium in 1975. He and four others had a rather bad time, and as the second night started to draw in, with a good 30 hours paddling behind them, the wind blowing hard and the sea tumultuous, they set off flares and were picked up by a passing cruise liner. In 1976, with much less publicity, they succeeded in crossing in good weather with little difficulty apart from weariness. Sod's Law, as usual, ensures that the public hears only about the spectacular failures and not about the successes won by hard work and enthusiasm.

Choice of Canoe

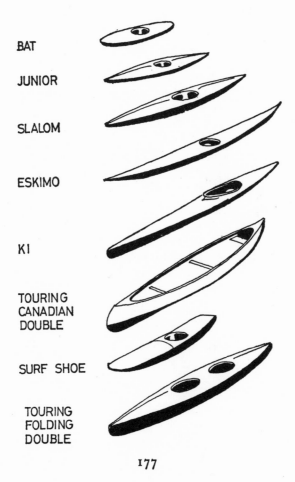

BAT

JUNIOR

SLALOM

ESKIMO

K1

TOURING
CANADIAN
DOUBLE

SURF SHOE

TOURING
FOLDING
DOUBLE

Appendix I

One basic question that all new canoeists will ask is; 'what canoe or kayak will suit my needs?' The answer is that only experience will tell, even though that isn't much help now. The following chart represents some of the better known canoes and kayaks in use today, with their approximate prices and a very brief description of their qualities in code form.

KEY TO THE CODE
The first part gives the source. The second part gives the approximate cost in pounds for a new boat at the time of writing, the third part gives several symbols which represent the chief characteristics, and the fourth part indicates the likely durability and resale value after two years.

Source, and price new		Commercial	C
		Kit	K
		G.R.P. (Amateur)	G

Qualities.	Stable laterally	Sl
	Stable directionally	Sd
	Manoeuvrable	M
	Fast	F
	Fun	Fu
	Competition	C
	Load Carrying	L
	Basic training	B
	Surf stunts	Ss
	Deep sea	D
	River	R

Durability. Number of years (Usual usage) Y4
Value in Pounds (after 2 years) V15

Type	Length	Beam	Weight	Code
BAT	7 ft. 6 in.	22 in.	20 lb.	C/56/M-Fu-B-C/Y2-V15 . . . or G/20/ditto/Y2-V10
Junior	11 ft.	22 in.	18 lb.	C/60/Sl-M-Fu-B/Y4-V25 . . . or G/18/ditto/Y4-V15
Slalom	13 ft. 6 in.	24 in.	28 lb.	C/75/M-C-Fu-B/Y2-V45 . . . or G/25/ditto/Y2-V35 . . . or K/16/ditto/Y2-V10
Eskimo	17 ft.	22 in.	35 lb.	C/140/D-Ss-Sd-F/Y5-V85 . . . or G/45/ditto/Y5-V65 . . . or K/18/ditto/Y4-V15
K1	18 ft.	19 in.	28 lb.	C/400/F-Sd-C-R/Y10-V350 . . . or G/30/ditto/Y5-V45
Touring Canadian Double	16 ft.	32 in.	50 lb.	C/120/L-R-Sl-M/Y10-V85 . . . or K/40/ditto/Y5-V60
Surf shoe	10 ft.	24 in.	35 lb.	C/65/Fu-Ss-M/Y3-V25 . . . or G/25/ditto/Y3-V20
Touring Folding Double	17 ft.	30 in.	55 lb.	C/approx. 200/L-R-D-Sd-Sl/Y10-V150
Surf ski Solo Comp	18 ft.	22 in.	30 lb.	C/85-115/Y2-V45

This rough guide is an outline that applies at the time of writing. However. The canoeing world contains many, many popular designs, and so this very brief list only includes the very few main types. For example, the slalom type C1 and C2 are in much more frequent use now than they were five years ago; and in another five years time they may well be even more popular.

179

Books About Canoeing

It is quite surprising, the number of books that are available about canoeing. I have over forty on my shelves alone. To list all these would be superfluous. However, I will recommend a few for certain special reasons.

Living Canoeing, Alan W. Byde, A. & C. Black. Because I wrote it, and because it was the best advice I could then give, and my views haven't altered much since 1968, when it was written.

Canoeing Complete, Sutcliffe and Skilling, Kaye books. A collection of chapters by people skilled in their own branch of canoeing. Again, my chapter on canoe building is some of the best advice I can give in a small space. The third edition contains a new chapter based on glass-reinforced plastic work, and this is the essence of a further book I am to write, to be called 'Build Your Own Canoe', or something like that. Canoeing Complete also contains an excellent bibliography. The book is available as I write, and most libraries have it, or will obtain it.

The Bark Canoes and Skin Boats of North America, Adney and Chappelle, Smithsonian Institute, Washington. A beautiful book, a true source book.

British Coracles and Irish Curraghs, James Hornell, Society for Nautical Research, National Maritime Museum, Greenwich. A favourite browsing book for me. Tells me much about the origins of the use of rivers and sea in Britain.

Surf and Sea, John M. Kelly, Barnes, New York. An excellent book on surfboard design and use, with exciting pictures.

Hawaii, James A. Mitchener. Chapter two, 'Navigation of a Polynesian Sea going Canoe', puts present-day long voyages in clear perspective.

Greenland, Vol 2, 1928, Commission for the Direction of the Geological and Geographical Investigation in Greenland, Humphrey Milford, London. A wonderful book on Eskimos, kayaks, myths, seal hunting, and so on in Greenland up to forty-five years ago.

Canoe Building in GRP, Alan Byde, A. & C. Black. A good book on canoe building in grp. Read in conjunction with . . .

Canoe Design and Construction, Alan Byde, Pelham. The only book I know of in the English language which tells you how to set about designing your own canoe.

Sea Canoeing, Derek Hutchinson, A. & C. Black. This is a recent book and just about the only one which deals solely with sea kayaking. Techniques, equipment, and constructional methods are dealt with here, plus some good stories on canoeing at sea.

Aboriginal Bark Canoes of the Murray Valley, Robert Edwards, South Australian Museum, Rigby, 1975. It is a little esoteric by the standards of this book, yet nevertheless quite fascinating.

Man and the Sea, Philip Banbury, Book Club Associates, London, 1975. An excellent book on how Man got about in the seas and waters around Britain from the ice age to the Norman conquest. Something for the canoeist in this.

These are only a few of the books I have had the pleasure to read. If I were to advise a candidate for the B.C.U. Senior Coach examination what three books to read, I would advise, this one (or *Living Canoeing*), *Canoeing Complete*, and the set of booklets by the B.C.U. or the *Coaching Manual*, also obtainable from the B.C.U.

Some Useful Addresses

For information about clubs in your area:
British Canoe Union, 70 Brompton Road, London, SW3 1DT.
Addresses of canoe manufacturers: An up-to-date list is obtainable from the British Canoe Union.
Canoeing magazine is obtainable from the Editor, The Chapel, 19 Main Street, Hemington, Derby, DE7 2RB.
For information about public courses, nationally:
National Sports Council, 70 Brompton Road, London, SW3 1DT.

Index